Crossing
ALL BOUNDARIES

It Can Happen to You–
Whatever *It* Is

JOE BRADLEY

First Large Print Edition

For contact information:

Joe Bradley

LeanonmebyJoe.com

ISBN: 978-0-9969382-1-1

Set in 18 pt. ITC Galliard

Printed in the United States of America

JS
&S

Publishing

DEDICATION

I dedicate this to my wife, Sherry, who has stood patiently by me as I spent the time needed to complete this book. Thank you, dear, for the encouragement and comfort you have provided in tough times and for standing strong through the trials we have faced.

I also dedicate this to our children, including our sons-in-law, daughter-in-law, and grandchildren who are a part of what is written here.

In addition, I dedicate this to all military veterans, those who have struggled with suicidal ideations, and the nearly five million families that have been touched by the suicide of a family member. I pray that God will guard your heart and mind and that not one more family will have to experience the excruciating pain associated with the suicide and loss of a loved one.

ACKNOWLEDGEMENTS

I want to give special thanks to those who have encouraged the writing of this book. Thank you Mark Johnson, Kay Vinci, and Bob Salinas for reading the initial manuscript and offering me your valuable insight.

I thank my family members who have given their input and reminded me of the things they remembered and thought were important.

Thank you Dan Gardner, Ken Dunlap, Roger Brock, Ted and Cheryl Koon, and Donna Cantrell for all the time you spent with me in ministry.

I thank my niece, Holly Thorpe, her coworker, Jason Ryan, and her friend, Stephanie Burt, for their willingness to share the lessons learned in publishing.

I will always be indebted to those who guided and supported me during my years in the U.S. Army. Thank you for encouraging, believing in, and desiring the very best for me.

I also thank all those who trained and helped me to function as a blind person and always expected the most out of me.

Thank you Rev. Tommy Reeves and everyone at Christian Life Church. You have all been a blessing to my family and me.

I want to acknowledge the invaluable assistance I received from Deb Williams. She not only edited the book but also guided me through the steps along the way. She was always willing to make adjustments and share the knowledge and words of wisdom she has gained over the years.

Michael Carter has generously given of his time and talent to see this book through to its completion. He has designed the cover, the format, and layout for the book in regular and large print as well as for an EBook. He is a library of information and help for those who need it. He and Deb Williams are two resources that are as instrumental in the publishing of *Crossing all Boundaries* as I am. I encourage you to contact Michael and plug-in to the seemingly unending knowledge and talent he possesses. Michael can be contacted by email: mrcarter56@gmail.com and Deb by email: debwilms@aol.com

Table of Contents

Foreword

We learn much about life through the lives of others. We understand more about the compassion, faithfulness, and grace of our Heavenly Father as we see it working in the lives of those closest to us. It produces the strength, courage, and perseverance we need to walk in His way and ultimately be restored to His will for our lives. As you read this book, you will see life, even Kingdom life, is not for the faint of heart. However, encouragement is to be gained by understanding the life of this man, Joseph Bradley.

Much of the life of Joe Bradley is revealed in this book, *Crossing all Boundaries*. As the title might indicate, there is not much that challenges the courage of this man, nor holds him captive by the consequences that have resulted from choices in life. The words of Joe's testimony confirm all we know about our Heavenly Father and His Words of life to us. We can learn much about life through Joe's experiences and how the Heavenly Father so loved this man that His plan was worked out in his life in such a way that it is an encouragement to us all.

Joe Bradley, the man we have come to know and appreciate, has become one of Father's precious sons, who through his dedication and determination to finish well has by his words and deeds accomplished much. Just as when he was as a member of the armed forces, he pressed to be all that he could be for his country, his desire now is to be all Father would want him to be in the Kingdom. To understand the story of Joe's life confirms to our hearts that Father has purpose for all of us, regardless of how often we fail to walk closely to Him. His grace will always restore us to His Way and His Will as we respond to His Heart.

I trust as you read Joe's life story that it will stir up the same courage and determination that allows Joe to stand in front of many groups and congregations, and transparently share his life just as he has in this book. May his life, insights, and commitment to walk close to Jesus be an encouragement to us all.

Pastor Tommy Reeves,

Missions Pastor

Introduction

There aren't many people in this world that haven't been touched by a tragedy of some type. In life there are going to be good times and bad times, laughs and tears, celebrations and sorrows, births and deaths, marriages and divorces, moments that make us proud and moments that bring pain. There will be times of reward and times we believe we were treated wrongly. We will experience acceptance and rejection, wins and losses, understandings and misunderstandings, agreements and disagreements, times of closeness and times of separation. We will have times to speak and times to be silent. There will be times when our vote brings about a desired outcome and times when it doesn't.

There are situations in life that happen to everyone. We can live in a mansion, under a bridge, or be imprisoned. We may be rich, famous, beautiful, handsome, strong, intelligent, persuasive, well liked, and have the ability to purchase whatever we desire. On the other hand, we may be poor, unknown, dirty, weak, uneducated, lack verbal skills, rejected by society, and wonder where our next meal is going to come from.

We may be the President, the First Lady, a prime minister, king, queen, Indian Chief, or a tribal leader. We may have the use of all parts of our body and senses, or we may be handicapped in some way; young or old, in good health or ill, have family or be alone, own a business, or work at a car wash. We may be in the military; an officer, warrant officer, or enlisted service member. We may be an inventor or work for the government, a singer or actor, a dad, mom, a son, or daughter. We may be a clergy person, medical doctor, psychologist, judge, police officer or a gang member. We may be an adolescent, teenager, young adult, or over forty. We may be an orphan, single parent, or widowed. We may have a car, a four-wheeler, a boat, jet ski, airplane, and own an island.

The country in which we live may be democratic, socialist, communist, or a kingdom. We may flee from one country to another or stay in one place all our life. We may live in the mountains, a cave, an igloo, the jungle, swamp, on a reservation, or by the ocean.

We may be American, African, Chinese, Cuban, German, Indian, Israeli, Jamaican, Japanese, Korean, Mexican, Russian, Spanish, or some other nationality.

No matter who we are, what we have, who we know, how many people know us, how great a singer or an actress, how well educated, what we do, where we live, what we can afford or how influential we are, there are tragic things that happen to people in all nationalities, cultures, races, professions, at all ages, and in all places. What has happened to others can also happen to us. Tragedy crosses all boundaries.

This book explains some of the tragic events that have happened in my life. It also includes information that can help anyone who is experiencing similar situations. I truly hope it will be beneficial to you and others you know.

Chapter

1

The Early Years

I was born November 12, 1955, and am the youngest of four. I have two brothers and a sister. When I was about four years of age, my mom and dad divorced. My mom worked in a sewing plant, at different cafés, and in a furniture mill. She raised the four of us on her own. Her weekly pay rarely met the needs of a family our size, and most of the time we lived from day to day. We moved at least eight times before I got out of Junior High School.

Divorce, mom working all the time, and the lack of a dad pushed my two older brothers and sister to take on responsibilities that weren't meant for them. Unfortunately, when adults get a divorce, or have issues with alcohol or drugs, oftentimes the older children are forced into this role. I am thankful that God gave me the brothers and sister He did.

My sister Faye and I often visited mom while she worked at one of the cafés. When we did, even though I was painfully shy, we were normally asked to do the "twist" for the customers. The "twist" was a popular dance during that time (late 50s and early 60s).

I went to kindergarten at a recreation center located behind our house. I remember the times I was corrected with a ruler on my hand and soap in my mouth. Of course, I was always wrongly accused with no right to a lawyer, trial, or method of appeal. My teachers were the judge, jury, and executioners.

On the day that kindergarten graduation was held, I didn't receive a diploma because my birthday was past the deadline to go to 1st grade that year. I was heartbroken and cried from the recreation center to our house, so mom decided she would go back and talk with my teachers. She came back with a solution that the three of them came up with—she handed me half a diploma. I can laugh about this now and thank God for a mom who did the best she could with what she had.

It was not uncommon for me to be outside playing from early in the morning until dark. The neighborhood kids and I played marbles, hopscotch, jumped rope, kicked tires down the street, and made stilts to walk with. We also played with sling shots, hula hoops, yo-yos, paddle balls, cap guns, climbed trees, played army and cowboys and Indians. Our horses were made of tree limbs and broomsticks. We would also play dodge ball, red rover, hide-n-seek, horseshoes, and try to roll barrels with our feet while standing on them. In those days, there wasn't a fear of children being harmed or abducted.

The center had card games, checkers, dominos, croquet, and various board games we could check out and use. They had Popsicle sticks and glue, items to make potholders and to string beads. Outside the center there were swings, seesaws, a merry-go-round, a slide, monkey bars, a pool about a foot deep, a basketball court, and a baseball field.

The bookmobile came to the center once or twice a month. We could check out books and keep them until the next time they came. My favorite books were those by Dr. Seuss, like *Green Eggs and Ham* and *Cat in the Hat*. Do you remember these, "Sam I Am?"

I have fond memories of adults sitting on their porches in the evening enjoying talking. Things didn't seem to be so fast paced back then. If an adult saw a child doing something wrong, they would normally correct them. If necessary, they would tell their parents who in-turn would thank the person for letting them know. This always turned out to be double trouble.

Adults, teachers, police officers, and others in authority were usually shown the respect they were due. It was not uncommon for a judge to offer a person the option of joining the military or being sentenced for their crime. I also heard a judge give two people the opportunity to attend church services and to return the next week for their judgment.

Our telephone was the rotor style, and we were connected to a party line, which meant that several houses on our street had the same connection. We would often pick up the phone to find someone already talking on it and have to wait our turn. The lines were above ground on telephone poles, which made it dangerous to talk on the phone during a thunderstorm. I was standing on the patio at the center when my teacher was talking on the phone during a storm. Lightning struck the phone and knocked her down on the cement floor. Thankfully, she didn't incur any major injuries.

The television we owned could only show programs in black and white. I recall a plastic piece the size of a television screen that had green on the bottom, clear in the center, and blue across the top. This was placed on the screen to give an illusion of a semi-color picture. There were only four channels available. We used rabbit ears and outside antennas for better reception.

The favorite programs for kids back then were cartoons like Mickey Mouse, Donald Duck, Smokey the Bear, Road Runner, Popeye, and Mighty Mouse. We also enjoyed the Three Stooges, Little Rascals, Bonanza, Gunsmoke,

Roy Rogers, Daniel Boone, Star Trek, Lost in Space, Red Skelton, and Disney programs. During those days, parents didn't have to be concerned about what a child would hear or see on the TV. When profanity was used for the first time on television, I remember people laughing about it. I don't know if they were laughing from the shock of it or just that it gave them something to talk about.

Christmas was a special time. We always had a live tree, decorated with lights the size of a small light bulb. They were colored in red, yellow, blue, green, and white. I would come home from school, lie down on the couch, and look at the colors reflecting off the ceiling. The tree was decorated with tensile and ornaments. We used the white spray on the windows and wrote Merry Christmas. On Christmas

Eve, we would go to bed early so Santa could come. We always hoped for snow, but the little we occasionally got was during January or February.

When I was around ten years old, I was standing near a fire hydrant in front of our house when I was shocked to have an overwhelming thought, "I just want to die." I knew something was wrong with that.

My best friend was Earl Blackmon. Earl and I spent time at Odom's Grocery, which was located at the end of our street where we would shoot pool. Someone had the jukebox playing most of the time. It held 7-inch records with a single song recorded on each. Albums were recorded on 10 and 12-inch records. Most homes had record players. The radio was our means of listening to music in the car until eight track tapes and tape players came along.

After Earl and I grew up we found out that our mothers had also been best friends when they were young but had lost track of each other after getting married.

My Boxing Career

As a teenager I boxed, but the only trophy I received is from 1970 that says "Runner Up"—there were only two of us in the match. I once had a t-shirt that said, "If you are losing the game, change the rules." My mom, older brother and sister-in-law, drove for three hours to see me box in a match that lasted at best 30 seconds— no I was not the winner. That was one of those times where I thought "get them off of me." I did enjoy boxing and I learned each time I boxed. Hey, what's pain without gain? Joe Frazier said, "Ali always said I would be nothing without him. But what would he have been without me?"

School Didn't Really Matter

I raked yards and sold peanuts using my bicycle and a basket that slid over the handlebars. I also worked at a curtain factory, gas station, at Hardees, and at Good Year Tire Store. At sixteen I dropped out of High School and went to work as a carpenter's helper. It was during this time that I decided to join the Army. My dad served during WWII and both my brothers served in Vietnam.

CHAPTER

2

In the Army Now

In December 1973 I arrived at Fort Jackson, S.C. where I went through Basic Combat Training (BCT). I recall how nice the drill sergeants were while at the reception station. We were given a free one-style-fits-all haircut and free clothes, hats, shoes, and boots along with all the amenities. We also received all the equipment needed to play army. Then we loaded on the bus and were taken to a field close to our barracks. The drill sergeant told us in a tone you would use when talking to a baby, NOT, GET OFF THE BUS!!! He had us running around the field, picking up and putting down our duffle bags, and performing various exercises. He then gave us five minutes to get to our barracks, put our bags on our bunk, and get back down in formation. The fun had started.

We learned to march, run in formation, salute, exercise as a platoon, make a bunk military style, polish brass and boots, how to wear our uniforms properly, clean barracks, and pick up trash and cigarette butts. We attended classes to learn first aid, all about our M16 rifle, the code of conduct, how to perform guard duty, and numerous other topics. We learned about nuclear, biological, and chemical warfare. We went through the gas chamber and had to take off our mask and say our name, rank, and social security number. After we did, they allowed us to exit the building. Our eyes were watering, and we were coughing and gagging, and then told each other that it wasn't that bad.

We also went to the different ranges to become proficient with our M16; to throw grenades; to use grenade launchers; an M60 machine gun; and a weapon called the LAW, which is used to immobilize a tank. We were instructed on how to locate a mine, dig foxholes, and set up fields of fire. We went through obstacle courses where we walked logs, jumped trenches, climbed walls, and used ropes to maneuver.

I also attended Advanced Individual Training (AIT) at Fort Jackson where I learned to perform as a Clerk Typist. My first assignment was with HHD, 67th Maintenance Battalion at Fort Benning, GA. I served as the company clerk (hello radar). My roommate was

Sergeant Bill Cross of Cross, S.C. We traveled home together as often as we could.

President Ford took the opportunity to visit Fort Benning and attended a demonstration put on by the Cadre at the Ranger school. The units were asked to send volunteers to fill up the bleachers for the demonstration. The unit leaders reminded us that we volunteered when we joined the Army.

Getting Married

I met my wife-to-be, Ethel, on one of my visits home to Sumter, S.C. where I grew up. Her father was a retired Air Force Veteran. In early 1975, I asked her to marry me. My sister had come to know the Lord a couple years before this, and it was her pastor who I asked to perform our wedding ceremony.

However, before he would agree, he wanted to talk with the two of us.

My Need for Salvation

We went over to his home one morning and as we sat on the couch he asked, "Joe, if you were to die today, do you know for sure that heaven would be your home?" I told him, "No Pastor, I don't." He then opened his Bible and told me what it said in Romans 3:23: "For all have sinned, and come short of the glory of God" (KJV). He went on to say that I needed to realize that I was a sinner and that everyone who has ever lived, besides Jesus Christ, is a sinner. I was then told that someone has to pay for those sins. I heard what the Bible says in Romans 6:23, "For the wages of sin is death, but the free gift of God is eternal life in Christ Jesus our

Lord." The pastor explained to me that if I choose to pay for my own sins that I will be eternally separated from God, but if I accept the payment that Jesus Christ made for me I would live with Him forever. I then heard how a person can be saved as the pastor read Romans 10:13, "for whosoever shall call upon the name of the Lord shall be saved" (KJV). Acknowledging the fact that I was a sinner and desiring God's mercy and forgiveness, I asked Him to forgive me of my sins and to come into my heart and save me.

Three Daughters in Three Assignments

After Ethel and I were married, we spent sixteen months in Germany where we had our first daughter, Karena. I was assigned to Company E, 708th Maintenance Battalion, in

Baumholder. I served as the company clerk under First Sergeant, later Command Sergeant Major, Donald Ransburg. He had also been my detachment sergeant at Fort Benning, GA. The First Sergeant and his wife, Gracie, cared for the three of us like we were family.

During my flight over a portion of Germany, while going in for the landing at the airport, I looked down and thought about how beautiful it was. It seemed to be manicured with fields laid out in a certain order. The grass was green and shining. There were times when the weather changed suddenly and you could see rain, sleet, snow, and sunshine all in the same day.

We lived in one of the small towns close to Baumholder. We stayed on the second floor of a house with the owner, Ms. Henn, living on the first floor. Our living room had a window with a view of a hill across the road. This is where I saw my first white Christmas. It was like a poster card. The children were playing together and sliding down the hill on their sleighs.

Ethel and I visited one of the broken down castles in a town nearby. There were carnivals that came through and events that were held that we were able to enjoy. We also participated in what is known as a volksmarch. This was a hiking event we went on with other soldiers and people in the community.

The military decided that they wanted everyone to have a High School diploma, so I attended classes during the day and received a diploma from Big Bend Community College. While I took these classes, I realized I enjoyed learning and I could do what was required. I don't remember anyone ever talking about college when I was young.

I reenlisted in the Army in December 1976 and elected to change my Military Occupation Specialty (MOS) to that of a company clerk, which would allow me to be promoted to E-5 ninety days after the school was completed. During my next assignment, I appeared before a promotion board and was placed on the E-6 Promotion Standing List.

I arrived at Fort Jackson, S.C. in early 1977 where my wife and I had our second daughter, Sabrina, and was assigned to 4th Platoon,

498th Medical Company (Air Ambulance) located at the Columbia Metropolitan Airport. When I first arrived, we occupied two areas in the old terminal building. It was one story with a set of stairs on one side where you could go up on the roof to wave and see the planes takeoff. Later there was a new hangar and offices constructed, and with General Jimmy Doolittle present, it was dedicated in his honor.

The Slogan for the Army during that time was, "BE ALL YOU CAN BE IN THE ARMY." Our middle daughter later came up with her own version and it said. "BE ALL YOU CAN BE, WITH AN UGLY WIFE AND A MESSED UP LIFE, IN THE ARMY." Her mom didn't care for that version.

During my time stationed at Fort Jackson, my family and I got in a good church. I was part of the visitation ministry where I would go out once a week and tell people about Jesus Christ and invite them to church. I was also part of the bus ministry and would go out on Saturday to visit the children to tell them I loved them and asked if they were coming to church the next morning. Then on Sunday morning I would get the bus to pick up the children. They would come out of their homes in the best clothes they had, get on the bus, put their arms around me, and tell me they loved me. I don't think a gold medal can be compared to a child full of love, putting their arms around you and telling you they love you.

In late 1979 there were four

members of the unit who decided to take the Flight Aptitude Test. If they passed, they were going to apply for Helicopter Flight Training. My Commander, Captain, later Lieutenant Colonel, Robert Whiting encouraged me to take the test as well. After a training session with one of the members taking the test, we all passed the exam and I prepared and submitted the applications. Everyone was accepted. I left Fort Jackson in early 1980 and proceeded to Fort Rucker, AL where my wife and I had our third and final daughter, Christina.

Helicopter Flight Training

I went through ten months of Helicopter Flight Training. I initially started in the Training Helicopter (TH55), a two-seater aircraft. One of the first procedures my instructor wanted me to learn was hovering (to keep the helicopter motionless while a certain height from the ground). When he turned the controls over to me, I couldn't keep the helicopter inside an area as big as a football stadium. My instructor would take the controls and with two fingers, hold the aircraft completely still. I was made to put a pencil over my middle finger and under my index and ring fingers. This was to let me know how hard I was trying to grip the cyclic, which is the control used to travel forward, backward, left and right. It took several flights, but one day it clicked. What a day that was! I later trained in the Huey Utility Helicopter (UH-1), which was the Vietnam era aircraft.

The school was intense and exciting.

We were constantly learning new information. We had classes part of the day, and flight training the other part. We were tested on each subject matter. We would study in between classes and any time we could find time to do so. As a Warrant Officer Candidate, I was required to live in the barracks for several months.

We were taught all about the different aircraft we flew in. We learned the systems such as electrical, engine, fuel, transmission, main and tail rotors, hydraulics, emergency procedures, radios, instruments, the flight controls, etc. We also learned about flight procedures, filing flight plans, getting weather reports, and what type conditions were suitable for flying. We took classes that informed us about the various clouds, weather patterns, inversions, problems with ice forming on the blades, and more. We were taught to fly the aircraft without looking outside and only using the aircrafts instruments.

We learned how to enter the flight pattern at airports, to take down flight instructions from the tower, and how to move from one area to another for takeoff or after landing. We trained to fly at night and land in an area with portable lights set up in a field. Additionally, we practiced flying at low level, a procedure whereby you maintain a constant altitude and airspeed while flying closer to the earth. We also flew contour, maneuvering the aircraft in accordance with the contour of the earth while maintaining a constant airspeed and nap of the earth (NOE), adjusting altitude and airspeed in accordance with vegetation and obstacles, weather and ambient light, to shield ourselves from being seen by the enemy. There were times that the blades were above the trees and the aircraft fuselage was just below the tops.

Emergency procedures along with the various aircraft limits had to be memorized. We practiced some of them and would perform autorotation's taking the aircraft to the ground and landing safely. During training, the instructor pilot would cut the amount of power coming from the engines. The blades would continue to rotate and the aircraft had to be landed without the engine's assistance. One instructor had us perform auto-rotations until it almost became secondhand.

Fort Bragg, North Carolina/ Death Can Come Without Warning

Upon completion of flight school I was appointed as a Warrant Officer One and assigned to Fort Bragg, N.C. The unit transitioned from the UH-1 aircraft to the Sikorsky aircraft (UH-60). This was like going from a dune buggy to a limousine.

During this assignment I saw time after time how death could come without warning. I remember a soldier who was sitting down at breakfast one morning while on a field training exercise, and a fellow soldier's M16 fell and discharged and shot him in the back. By the time we could get to him, he had already met his destiny. I also remember a lady who ran off the bridge and the water was too deep for us to get to her.

Then I remember a crew picking up a Colonel, who was one week from retirement that was out skydiving on the weekend and his parachute failed to open, and he retired before he had planned to.

In 1983, while I was still at Fort Bragg, N.C., my brother-in-law and sister were involved in a wreck. They were pulling out of a parking lot one evening on a rural road when a car hit them in the side. My brother-in-law was thrown from the car and killed.

Embry-Riddle Aeronautical University

The unit I was assigned to, 57th Medical Detachment (RG), the original DUSTOFF, (Dedicated Unhesitating Service To Our

Fighting Forces), had twenty-four hour standby seven days a week. If I wasn't on duty, I was attending college at night and on the weekends because God was no longer an active part of my life. It was not that I told God that I didn't want Him to be a part of my life; it was that I allowed my life to become so busy that I didn't take time for Him to be a part of it. Does this sound familiar? I want to share my heart and tell you that if we aren't serving God where we are, we are not going to serve Him when we get to where we believe we are going. Why? Because over a period of time, knowingly or unknowingly, our life will become all about us and our pursuits. When our priorities with God get out of order, everything in our life gets out of order.

I Want a Divorce

I recall going home one day, while at Fort Bragg, walking in my house, and my wife, Ethel, was standing there. She took off her wedding rings, placed them in my hand, and told me she wanted a divorce—that she didn't love me anymore.

I, without a doubt, could have been a better husband and dad. I certainly lacked in a lot of areas, but her desire for a divorce broke me. For three days and nights I cried and prayed and begged God to allow me to keep my family, and He did allow me to keep them at that time. It was at this point in my life that I realized what God meant when He says, "they shall become one." I felt as if my heart was being ripped in half.

Just prior to this occurring and after completing my college degree, I had been discussing with my Detachment Commander the possibility of applying for a direct commission in the Medical Service Corps. He was extremely supportive of me and knew the time for the board was getting close. He called me into his office and told me I needed to make a decision before the cutoff date. I chose to apply.

Operation Urgent Fury

In December 1983, while a Chief Warrant Officer Two, I was commissioned as a Second Lieutenant in the Medical Service Corps and sent to Grenada, West Indies. The Detachment Commander had led a large portion of the unit's personnel there in late October during what was known as Operation Urgent Fury. They were sent to support the operation and the rescue of the medical students whose lives were in danger.

The remainder of the unit followed three days later, and flew into Barbados and stayed in abandoned buildings close to the airport. By this time our forces had things under control and President Ronald Reagan in his decisiveness had restored much of the prestige and dignity that our military was once afforded.

During the first of my two one-month stays in Grenada, Operation Urgent Fury switched to The Caribbean Peacekeeping Force and a portion of military personnel remained there for a period of time.

The people in Grenada were very appreciative and treated us with kindness. Some of the residents lived in wooden structures close to the ocean that were elevated from the ground and had ladders they used to get up and down.

The U.S. soldiers went into the communities and provided medical care and other services. At Christmas, boxes of stuffed animals were flown in and given out to all the children. The families were extremely grateful.

Korea and the Demilitarized Zone (DMZ)

I left Fort Bragg, N.C. and arrived in Seoul, Korea sometime in August 1984 where I served as a Section Leader in 1st Platoon, 377th Medical Company (AA) and had the mission of covering the Demilitarized Zone. I also served as the Platoon Leader of 4th Platoon, under the 377th Medical Company (AA) Commander, Captain, later Lieutenant Colonel, Dennis Duffey, which had the same mission. Additionally, I served as the Personnel Officer and Adjutant of the newly formed evacuation battalion, 52nd Medical Battalion (Provisional).

Our Platoon would fly to Camp Casey and stay a week at a time. The pilots had to study the map and memorize the Demilitarized Zone, which extended for more than 150 miles so that no matter where we would come up on it, we would know where we were. On each side of the DMZ there was a boundary, and I knew that as long as I flew down the center of the DMZ and stayed within those boundaries, everything would be all right. I also had the knowledge that if I were to fly to the north of those boundaries, I had an enemy who was prepared to shoot me down.

God's Map and Boundaries for Our Lives

I would like to tell you about God's map for our lives. It is called the Bible, and in it we can find the Demilitarized Zone or what we call the straight and narrow. We can find the boundaries that God set for our lives, and we need to understand that as we skirt the edge of these boundaries or occasionally step out that we too have an enemy, walking around as a roaring lion, seeking whom he may devour.

My First Korea Mission

My first mission in Korea occurred during my initial trip to Camp Casey. There had been a skirmish at Panmunjom when a North Korean visitor fled across the DMZ to South Korea and our soldiers, along with Korean Augmentees to the USA, engaged in a gun battle with North Korean Soldiers. An American soldier had been shot in the jaw and required immediate medical care and hospitalization.

Every place my family and I were stationed, we tried to take advantage of the sites and recreation areas close to us. We truly enjoyed our stay in Korea. We resided in a government contracted housing area. There were several facilities located there for us to use, including a gym, recreation center, tennis courts, playground, pool, craft shop, wood shop, a cafe, commissary, and chapel.

The children were always out playing and enjoying themselves. Ethel taught conversational English, and we spent time with some of the Korean students. We went to their homes, stayed in one of their apartments at an amusement park, took some of them to events on post, and the children took piano, guitar, and dance.

There was a gate going out the back of the area. We would walk to the shopping area in downtown Seoul. There were trampolines on one of the side streets that the girls would pay to jump on. On the way we would pass a business named "Kenturkey" Fried Chicken. Many of the vendors in Seoul had carts and parked them on the sidewalk where they would set up shop. The Korean people were very talented.

The girls went to jump on the trampolines and came across a man selling dogs. They came back to the house telling us about it and we agreed for them to have one. They chose the one they wanted and named him Colors. He was a small dog with a curly tail, and his hair was several different shades of brown, red, black, and white.

While in Korea, my family and I got back in church, but it was as if I never knew God to begin with. I reasoned about getting certain things out of my life thinking I could get close to God again, but as I spoke with the chaplain one day, he reminded me of I John 1:9 where it says, "If we confess our sins, He is faithful and just to forgive us our sins and cleanse us from all unrighteousness" (NKJV).

There were many times during my assignment in Korea that I found myself to be irritable, short-tempered, and snapping at those I was talking with. I hated when it happened. I couldn't understand why this was occurring, as I did not like being that way. I can only assume that I was in one of the stages of what would later become more mental and emotional pain than I had ever experienced.

My Last Military Assignment

During this assignment I was promoted to Captain. I departed Korea in December 1987, and after attending the Officer Advanced Course at Fort Sam Houston, Texas and Fort Rucker, Alabama, I was assigned to Readiness Group Lee (R.G. Lee) located at Fort Lee, Virginia, where I served as a Medical Advisor to the Reserve and National Guard Medical Units throughout the State.

What I didn't realize was that this would become my last military assignment. I, along with two Sergeants First Class, visited the units during their monthly drills and their yearly two-week training periods, also known as Summer Camp. I gained a tremendous respect for our Reserve and National Guard personnel as many of them served their communities in similar capacities during the week and were knowledgeable and proficient in their field.

In early 1989 I was told that in June of 1990 I would be returning to the 4th Platoon, 498th Medical Company (Air Ambulance) to serve as the Operations Officer. The unit was still located at the Columbia Metropolitan Airport and assigned to Fort Jackson, S.C. However, from the time I was told about this there was something within me telling me that this would never happen.

In August or September of 1989, I attended the Combined Arms Services Staff School (CAS3) at Fort Leavenworth, KS. I felt in my heart that this would be the last military school I ever attended.

Photos

Joe
Around six
years old

Joe
Junior High
School

Joe & Siblings
Gene, Arthur,
Faye, and Joe
1964

Arthur, Joe, Faye, and Gene
with Mom

Joe
Germany, 1976

Joe
sitting at his desk thinking,
"I changed jobs so I could fly."

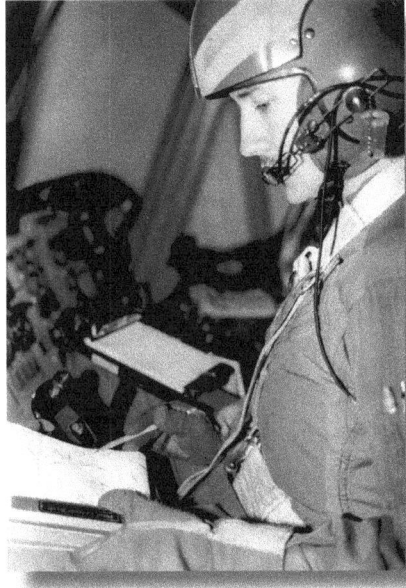

Joe
in aircraft
during a
mission,
looking over
flight data

Joe
Official
Military
Photo
1982

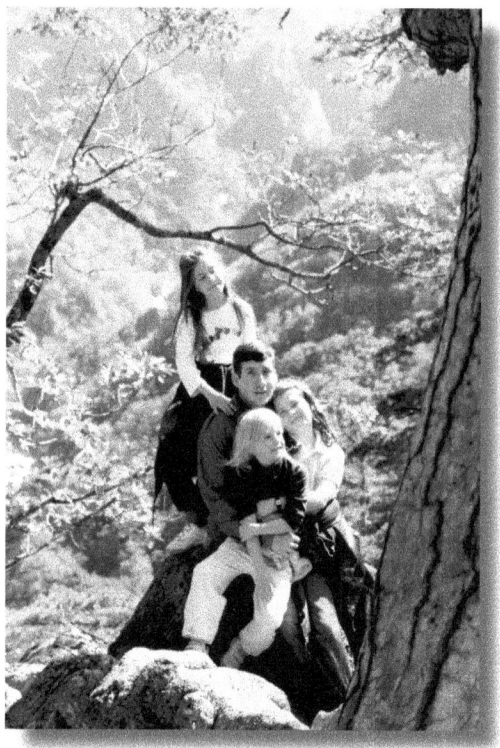

Joe
with Karena, Sabrina, and Christina
in Korea

Joe & Sherry
Wedding Day
21 Dec. 1997

Wesley, Sherry,
Joe, and Corey
Wedding Day

Joe &
Sherry
on a
cruise

Joe & Sherry
Visiting son
in California

Joe & Kip
Joe's first guide dog

Karena, Wesley, Sabrina,
Corey, and Christina

My Beloved Mother
16 July 1925 - 2 April 2014

CHAPTER

3

Losing All Hope

In early December 1989, while still at the school, I was in my room one evening when I felt cold spots on my lower back. It felt as if someone had put ice on me. I recall going to class the next morning and looking down at my papers to see that they were wet. I felt my forehead and saw that I was sweating. This was in the middle of winter. I finished the school and returned to Fort Lee, VA.

I went to the doctor about a half dozen times, and each time they would tell me that nothing was wrong. I remember the first visit when the doctor asked if I was depressed, and I told him "No," but that I was concerned. I later learned that his understanding of depression was not the same as mine (see Appendix B for a description of depression, Depression Symptoms and Warning Signs; Appendix C for suicide help, Dealing With Suicidal Thoughts and Feelings; and Appendix D for suicide prevention, How to Help Someone who is Suicidal).

The sweating never ceased and it got to where every bone in my body ached. I would lie down at night and every nerve in my body would shake. I had a constant desire to cry, and I wanted to sleep all the time. I would go to bed, wake up in the middle of the night, and couldn't go back to sleep, so I was always tired. I would go to work and all I could do was take off and ride around and cry and pray. I read my Bible and prayed for God to remove that thing from me. I have learned that God is not always going to remove my struggles. Sometimes God's answer to me is the same as God's answer to Paul in II Corinthians 12, where Paul talks about having a thorn in his flesh and he prays three times for God to take it away. God's answer to Paul was that His grace is sufficient and His strength is made perfect in weakness—our weakness. When Paul allowed God's strength to overcome his weakness, he later says, "I will glory in my weakness that I may rest in God's strength" (see II Corinthians 12:9). This is the same God who has and will strengthen us in our time of need.

I lost all interest in things I enjoyed. I had no desire for sexual intimacy. I lost a lot of weight because I didn't have an appetite. I withdrew from people, and though I thought many times about going to my Commander, I didn't because I couldn't put into words what I was experiencing. There was a pressure around my temple area and I was constantly rubbing my head. I lost all sense of purpose and goal in my life, and I began to feel hopeless and worthless. My brain was like a room with no windows and no doors. All I could do in that room in my mind was think. The more I would think, the smaller that room became until one thought was prevalent. That was, how do I get out of this?

Losing All Hope

The 28th of March 1990 was my wife's birthday, and I took her and the children out to eat that night. When I returned home, I opened my Bible one last time and read that God's grace is sufficient. I read that His mercy is from everlasting to everlasting, and I read that He would never leave me nor forsake me. But at that moment in my life, I felt God had forsaken me, and that's when I lost all hope.

"We are never defeated unless we give up on God."
~ President Ronald Reagan

29 March 1990

When I awoke the next morning, I hugged and kissed my wife and children and told them I loved them. I went off to work just like I normally did, and on the way to work I pulled into a recreation area on Fort Lee where we had previously enjoyed unit picnics.

I want to allow you to sit in the car with me that day. As I sat there, I wrote a note to Ethel and the girls. It read, "Ethel and Girls, I love you. I don't understand why I'm doing what I'm doing. Love, Joe and Dad." I placed that on the dashboard above the steering wheel. As I sat there, three thoughts came into my mind. The first was, "Joe, you need help." Second was, "Joe, if you ask for help, people are going to look down on you." The third was, "Joe, you know what you have to do, do it, and take it like a man."

Blinded But Not Abandoned

What happened next is something that I would have told others I'd never even consider. That's when I took a gun, cocked the hammer, placed it to the right side of my head and as I pulled the trigger, I said, "God, please help me."

I don't know how long I had been in the car when I thought I opened my eyes, but I couldn't see. I felt around in the car. I felt the dashboard, the windshield, and the steering wheel. Then I put my hand up to the right side of my head, felt that it was wet, and realized I was still alive. All I could do was lay my head back down, but as I did, God and His Word proved to be one—for He was in the car with me that day. I put my head back down and experienced what I can only describe as being a part of Jesus Christ and He a part of me. I can't think of anything I can do in this flesh that can be compared to what happened in that car. I know in John 14:20 the Bible tells us that Jesus is in the Father and

I am in Him and He is in me. This is what it was like.

After being in the car about four hours, God gave me the strength to get out of that car, and I started walking in the direction where I knew some apartments were located. Before I got to the apartments, I ended up inside a fenced in area with tennis courts. As I walked around the area, hanging onto the fence, a man saw me and came over and called for an ambulance. I remember the man asking me, "Who did this to you?" I responded, "I did." He said, "No, you didn't." He also contacted my unit and let them know what had happened.

When the ambulance arrived, I was taken to the emergency room at Fort Lee, then to the Medical College of

Virginia in Richmond, and eventually to Walter Reed Army Medical Center located in Bethesda, Maryland.

Walter Reed Army Medical Center

While there, they put a piece of cloth under my nose and told me they had to see if my brain was leaking fluid, and if so, they would have to do an emergency operation. A day or so later they took that piece of cloth from under my nose and told me I had lost my smell, my taste, and had severed my optic nerves and would never see again.

The first week or two, I lived on chocolate chip cookies and coffee. I gained 28 pounds going from 165 to 193 pounds. Ever since I have been struggling with getting back down and maintaining the weight I desire.

A doctor came to talk with me from the psychiatric ward and told me he wanted me to spend some time on that ward. My immediate thoughts were that I didn't want to be somewhere that people would be pulling at my clothes or touching me. Guess I had seen too much television. I also thought, "I'm not crazy, all I did was shoot myself."

When I was transferred to the psychiatric ward, I saw very quickly that the people there weren't any different. They all had struggles, like I did, that they were trying to get through.

I had members of R.G. Lee, the units I supported, my family, and friends, as well as members of the unit I was supposed to be assigned to come and visit me. Chief Warrant Officer Chris Middleton flew from

4th Platoon, 498th Medical Company (AA), Columbia, S.C., along with a medical evacuation crew. We had served together as enlisted soldiers with 4th Platoon, and both went to flight school at the same time.

Command Sergeant Major Fredricke Clayton was the Walter Reed Command Sergeant Major. He was also the Command Sergeant Major of the 52nd Medical Battalion (Provisional) when I served as the Personnel Officer and Adjutant. He came to visit me while I was on the psychiatric ward. I remember him just sitting there and listening. His presence spoke volumes, and was very comforting to me.

I prayed and asked God that He wouldn't allow me to have total darkness but that I could at least see light. As I was walking down the hall in the hospital, I thought I caught a glimpse of something passing me on my left side. Then it got to where I could distinguish when something was between me and a light source. I don't have that ability anymore, but what God has taught me is that He gives us exactly what we need, exactly when we need it.

I once heard a chaplain give an illustration of grace (God's unmerited favor). He said to picture a table sitting in the middle of a room as a life situation, and the air that surrounds the table and fills the room as God's grace. I can only tell you that my blindness and situations since have never been bigger than the strength, peace, and comfort God has supplied.

What Is It Like to Be Blind?

Though I know I am different, I don't really feel any different as a person than I did when I was sighted. When any of us have a big change, there are going to be those times of doubt, fear, frustration, grief, and uncertainty. There are times I feel separated from others. I have had many situations where I would speak to someone I knew was close to me, only to discover they were on the phone, looking the other way, or weren't sure if I was speaking to them. There are also times I don't realize someone is speaking to me. If I am in a room with others, but not talking directly with someone, I feel a little awkward. When I am talking with a person, they are more real to me, but the time I am best connected is when someone puts their hand on my shoulder, arm, or back and I can feel their presence.

It didn't take long to realize I had to learn how to function as a blind person. While in Walter Reed, I bent over to discover there was a table in front of me. I hit the edge of it with my nose and peeled back a portion of my skin. I have done likewise hitting bedposts, dressers, faucets, safety railing in showers, etc. I have learned to put my hand in front of my face before I bend over, but occasionally I still forget to do so and end up learning that lesson all over again.

This not only applies with bending over, it also applies to sitting down. When sighted, there's visual assurance that a chair is present, but I have to physically put my hand on the chair before I sit down. I learned this lesson when I returned home from Walter Reed. I went to sit down on our couch when my middle daughter asked me not to sit on her. I slipped over, sat down, and ended up on the floor. I didn't know she was sitting on the end of the couch.

I have been taught how to use a

stove safely. I learned the method for getting the pot/pan in the middle of the eye, which way to put the handle, how to mark the settings and basic cooking. Making beds, sweeping, mopping, washing dishes, vacuuming, dusting, washing windows, and other household tasks haven't been a problem for me. Washing and drying clothes and using the microwave simply require the use of braille dots to indicate the choices I can select. I iron my own clothes and know what setting I am on by lining up the markers that someone helps me put on.

I enjoy working with my hands, one of the methods I use to make up for the loss of my sight. I ask others to draw in the palm of my hand when describing the layout of a room, home, building, or property.

My hearing makes up for some of

the loss when I am given directions, descriptions, and instructions. Hearing is very useful when there are changes in sound. I can tell when there is a hallway, when I go under an overhang, if I am close to traffic, and so much more. My hearing also affords me the enjoyment and pleasure of noticing God's creation all around me. My desire is to hear spiritually and enjoy God's closeness and love for me.

The sensitivity of my feet, with my shoes on, helps tremendously when determining structure, grade, alignment, and texture.

Typing is like secondhand. Using the computer was something I had to learn as well as memorizing braille letters, numbers, symbols, and abbreviations. Then I had to write in braille and read by feeling the dots and interpreting what was being said.

I enjoy listening to books on my Victor Reader stream. I download books from book share and from the national library services. When watching a movie or going to a theater, someone will tell me the things I can't see, especially during the silent parts. There are movies with descriptive audio to play at home. Most theaters also have ear sets I can use to listen to the descriptive audio for the movie playing.

I used the cane when walking from place to place after being trained how to position the cane and told which side it should be on when my right or left foot is forward or back. This was initially a true test of walking by faith and not by sight. I now understand that walking by faith as a Christian is making a decision and learning to take God at His word and being obedient to what He says. I then need to trust God to help in my decisions and to give me direction, guidance, protection, provision, and all I require. The outcome is in His hands.

"Faith is taking the first step even when
you don't see the whole staircase."
~Rev. Martin Luther King, Jr.

It didn't take long for me to get a feel for the various information the cane was giving me. The floor, wall, door, chair, bed, nightstand, table, carpet, appliances, and other items all have a different feel.

There are times I use a sighted guide. I hold onto a person just above their elbow and tell them to walk naturally because I can feel what they are doing. When we come to a curb or steps, I ask them to tell me curb or steps up or down. When entering or exiting a door, I ask them to tell me if the door opens in or out to my left or right. If we should encounter an area too narrow for both of us to get through walking side by side, I ask them to put the arm I am holding behind their back, which tells me to get behind them. When we clear the area, they return their arm to the natural position and I return to their side.

The toughest part of blindness is the inability to drive. There are big changes to adjust for when your desire to go places or do the things you would enjoy depends on the availability and willingness of others. Projects I would like to do often have to wait until I can go out and get the materials I need. I have used those who work with the council on aging to go to different places. There is a company called DART (Dial a Ride Transportation) that assists with this as well. The bus system is another method of travel, but they don't have a route close to where I live.

My favorite training was in what is known as manual skills. This consists of leather crafts, copper tooling, making ceramic items, sheet metal work, small engine repair, when requested, and woodworking. I was taught to use the table saw which is known as a saw stop that is supposed to stop if I touched the blade with my hand, though I never found anyone in the shop willing to demonstrate this for me. I also worked with the plainer, edger, band saw, standup drill, and radial arm saw in addition to other machines.

I have a picture in my mind of what the girls look like, but I have never seen my wife, our sons, our sons-in-law, our daughter-in-law, or any of our grandchildren.

I have learned to see things through the eyes of my heart that can't be seen with the natural eye. If I were given the choice of seeing naturally or with the eyes of my heart, I wouldn't hesitate to choose those of my heart. Why? Because what really matters in a person is not their appearance, fashion, race, nationality, or position. It is their love for others, compassion, kindness, humility, gentleness, patience, mercy, forgiveness, and the acknowledgement that all of us are made in the image of God and after His likeness, and that no one is more or less important to God than another.

I have used the eyes of others to learn what is around me. If a person can say what they see, then I can see what they say. I've had people tell me that asking them to explain what an object looks like helps them to really see the details of an item that they are describing.

It is not uncommon for my sleep patterns to be out of rhythm with night and day. Two to three times a year I have to readjust my sleep to get back on track.

How important is it to be able to smell!

Smell is a very important sense. After a period of time, I lost the memory of how things smell. The fragrance of a rose, perfume, a cake, a Christmas tree, and all the wonderful smells that change with the seasons. I have to be extra cautious when using a stove, fireplace, candles, or items that plug into an outlet because I can't smell anything that is burning. The only way I will know is for someone to tell me or a smoke alarm alerts me.

What About the Ability to Taste?

I eat and drink just like others. Someone may tell me, by using clock positions, what is on my plate. If I am not told what I am eating, I may not be able to figure it out unless I can tell by structure. I can taste difference, so I like spicy foods. I lost track of how many times I have knocked over a drink, so I normally make sure to put my drink in a certain position on the table. When possible, I have my adult sippy cup, a cup with lid and straw.

Grooming is done by touch. I shave by using my left hand to ensure I'm doing a good job. I do the same when combing my hair.

Choosing clothes can be done in several ways. Someone can tell me what color my clothes are, the clothes can be marked to indicate the color, clothes that go together can be hung in a group, and now there are applications for the IPhone and other devices that indicate the color being scanned.

The IPhone has an application

known as voice-over that can be turned on in settings. This feature allows me to use the phone by swiping my index finger from left to right on the screen. It will read to me what I am on and then I can double tap with one finger to open the application. I can also open an application verbally.

Other applications I use are Money Reader, which tells me the amount of the bill money I am scanning, and Red Laser, which is another good resource for the sighted and blind. With this application I can scan a barcode in a store and it will tell me what the item is and the price. It can also tell me if there are stores nearby where I can get a better deal. The application allows for searches and indicates when there are deals around me.

When traveling, I can get directions on my IPhone or from the GPS on my braille note. With the GPS, I can create personalized routes that I travel frequently by vehicle or when walking.

Use It or Lose It

The saying "use it or lose it" applies to those items I once looked at the price when purchasing but no longer do. I lose track of the price of gas, oil, milk, eggs, etc. The reason for this is someone I am with normally puts the items in the cart and I just pay for them. I also have to think about the spelling of words to make sure I am using the correct word and spelling. I am also losing the memory of the sharpness of certain colors.

The Line-of-Duty Investigation and the Medical Board

A line-of-duty investigation had to be conducted. An officer from R.G. Lee was designated to conduct the investigation. He determined that what had happened was in the line-of-duty. What this meant was that I would be afforded the same opportunities as others who retire and be considered for a medical rating, which included benefits for my family members.

My Commander, his precious wife, and others at R.G. Lee ensured that my family and I were well taken care of. He also ensured that Ethel was provided a room on the grounds at Walter Reed. I had the opportunity to talk with him while at Walter Reed and expressed how I wish I had come to him or one of the other leaders while I was going through my struggle. I encourage you to reach out to someone and be honest with them. If you can't put what you are experiencing into words, please see the information on depression, Appendix B, and list the items shown there.

What's Next?

Since that time I have attended The S.C. Commission for the Blind as well as the Southeastern Blind Rehab Center at the VA Hospital in Birmingham, AL. I assure you this was one of the best things I could have done. At the S.C. Commission for the Blind, I was around people who had been blind all their life and those who were going blind gradually. I learned a lot from them. Immediately after leaving the Commission, I went to Birmingham where I was around other veterans. Many of them had been wounded from past wars and some were losing their sight from degenerative diseases. Being there was just like being in the military—there is a bond between veterans that can't be explained.

If I named all the people who helped me learn to function as a blind person it would require a chapter of its own. I can only express to those who did that I would have been at a loss without them. There were organizations that would visit us at the VA in Birmingham. They would entertain us in some way and bring food, drinks, and a big heart.

Children's Counselor for the Blind

From December 1991 to December 1992, I had the privilege of working with Ms. Elizabeth McKown as a counselor for blind children in several counties throughout our state. I found as much, if not more, zeal and desire in these children as in those with all their senses. They were smart, enthusiastic, fun-filled, and adventurous. They loved working with their hands and welcomed challenges. I also had the privilege at various times to work with blind adults. They too welcomed the challenges and worked hard to learn those skills that would help them at work, at home, or in performing everyday tasks.

I have been asked that if a person is blind from birth, can they understand color? I encourage people to ask questions and learn what a blind or any handicapped person is capable of. Most of the time blind children and adults, as well as those with any handicap, are only limited by the expectations of others. I encourage you to expect the same as you do of yourself and allow the person to explain how they can or why they can't do something. A person blind from birth doesn't have any frame of reference for color other than explaining to them what they see is considered black. I'm not sure, but some of them may see black as well as a lighter shade of dark grey as I do.

As a person who had the ability to see for thirty-four years, I dream in color and my brain wants to make sense of what has happened. I have times where things I have seen in the past will pop up as if I were looking at it right then. This has happened numerous times, and during some of these times I have had to be still until it would subside, as it took my complete attention.

A child born blind has to also be taught that there are things outside of them and their body—such as a ball, radio, person, etc. When playing with a ball or toy, if it should roll away or they lose track of it, they have to be taught that it is still there close to them and they can reach out and get it.

Columbia International University (CIU)

In August 1993, I began taking courses with CIU to attain a Master's Degree in Counseling. I had been issued a braille note, which some called a Speak-N-Spell, and a laptop with screen reader capabilities. It would read whatever I brought up on the computer screen, and I could work with my hearing just like people can with their sight. The VA afforded me two readers/tutors to assist me in taking notes, doing research, taking tests, studying, and whatever else needed to be accomplished. They would read books on tape for me to listen to. They were the backbone for my schooling. Words aren't adequate to express my gratitude to each of them. Thank you. I graduated in December 1997 with a degree in counseling.

Chapter

4

Sharing My Story

Dan Gardner, a friend of my brother Gene, heard about what happened. God had put it on his heart to start a lay evangelistic ministry. We went to numerous churches in South Carolina to share. I also had the honor of speaking with several FCA groups at middle and high schools. Additionally, I spoke with classes at CIU and with other college students. I also shared with AA and NA members, had the privilege of talking with the veterans at Southeastern Blind Rehab Center, troops at Fort Jackson, S.C., and going into some of the prisons to tell of the hope of the Gospel, and while on vacation at Lakewood Campgrounds in Myrtle Beach, S.C.

Roger Brock, Ken Dunlap, Ted and Cheryl Koon, and Donna Cantrell as well as other members of the church I was attending, would normally be there to share in music and song.

When The Head of the Family is Distracted

We all deal with our struggles in different ways. As the head of the family, I was so distracted with what had happened to me that I didn't see the needs my family members had. I will be honest to say I was lost and stuck in between the sighted and blind, the Army and civilian life, uncertainty and identity, feeling less than a man, learning what it meant to be blind, and how to function as a blind person. My frustration came out in anger against those closest to me.

Ethel and the girls were all devastated by what I had done and the changes that came with it. While I was struggling with the consequences of my actions, my family was struggling with their own issues. My wife grew up with her dad in the Air Force and our daughters were all born while I was in the Army. The military life is all they knew.

The girls had a tough time adjusting to the different environment they found themselves in. They, too, were frustrated and somewhat lost.

The Bowling League

In 1993 Ethel joined a bowling league and began to occasionally drink. This was the method she chose to cope with her struggles. She decided to leave home in April 1994, returned in June that same year, and left again in early 1995.

I filed for a divorce, which was finalized in December 1995. Ethel initially stayed in the area with a friend. Later she moved back to Sumter, S.C. and remarried. Additionally, in December 1995, I had two daughters come to me two days apart, neither of them being married, and tell me they were pregnant.

When Reality Sets In

The girls remained with me after their mom and I divorced. I heard both of them express their fears and concerns about being a mom. We went through the nine months together, and by God's grace, we saw two beautiful and healthy girls be born one month apart.

Since that time our daughters have married. Karena and her husband have four children. Their oldest child is in college. They also have a child in high school, one in middle school, and one in elementary school. Sabrina has two children from her first marriage. Her daughter just graduated from high school and her son is in the eighth grade.

Christina married into a blended family. Her husband had custody of his two children from a previous marriage. One is in the Army stationed in Germany, and the other is in college. They had one child together. He turned five years old in May.

Our two older daughters live within thirty minutes and the youngest one lives within walking distance. We stay in regular contact and see each other, when we can, between the grandchildren's scheduled activities.

Meeting Sherry

I spoke at Dutch Fork Baptist Church in mid-1997. Afterward, Sherry came up to meet me and introduced herself. One day after church, I asked for a ride home, but when we walked out of church, one of my daughters was there to pick me up. From that time on I would listen for Sherry's voice when I went to church and speak to her when I could. Several weeks or months went by when I decided to call and invite her to dinner.

The two of us went to eat at a pizza restaurant located in the old mill in Lexington, S.C. The pizza was good, but not nearly as good as my company.

The Proposal

We didn't date very long before I

asked Sherry to go with me to Jewelry Warehouse. I wanted to look around, of course, through her eyes. When we arrived, we got out of the car and walked around to the back of it. I then took her hand and asked her to marry me. She said, "Yes", and we proceeded in to Jewelry Warehouse where we purchased our wedding rings.

Wedding Day

Sherry and I set the date for December 21, 1997. She and I both had a house only two streets apart, so we agreed whichever one sold first, we would live in the other. We never had to put the houses up for sale because my daughter worked with a lady who was looking for a house to buy. I began moving furniture from my house to Sherry's. The weather was cold and misty, so on the wedding day I had laryngitis and needed a microphone around my neck to be heard while I said my vows. Rev.

Danny Hedgepeth performed our wedding ceremony. Our daughters served as the bridesmaids and two sons-in-law and one brother stood in as groomsmen. Sherry's best friend, Robin, was her maid of honor. My oldest brother, Arthur, stood as my best man. Our two sons, Wesley and Corey, both dressed in their Marine Blues, proudly walked their mom down the aisle and gave her away. Mary Stamey did a fabulous job as the wedding coordinator.

When the vows were over, the cake cut, the pictures taken, and the food eaten, Sherry and I stepped into a limousine and headed for Myrtle Beach where we stayed until December 23 when we gathered at Sherry's mom's house for Christmas. We completed our honeymoon in January 1998 when we flew to Knoxville, Tennessee and drove in the snow to Pigeon Forge, where we stayed for a week.

Our First Breakfast

At Myrtle Beach, we went to the motel restaurant and ate breakfast. Our waitress was the daughter of a pastor at a local church. There was one other couple in the restaurant at the time. When we asked for the bill, we were told that the couple, which had already left, saw us praying and wanted to buy our breakfast. Thank You, Lord.

The Blended Family

We now had three daughters, two sons, two sons-in-law, and two grandchildren. At one time we had two daughters, two sons, two grandchildren, and the two of us living in a three-bedroom house.

Our sons would sleep on the living room floor. The dining room was designated as a fourth bedroom, and at one time one of our sons was living in our 10x12 building that was built to be a shop. He is the one the others envied.

We have multiplied since that time and now have a total of twenty-eight family members that includes fourteen grandchildren and two great grandchildren. Wesley has a son who is fifteen years old. Corey married into a blended family. His wife has three children. Two of them are married and have a child each. They have a daughter who is eleven and they had a son together who will be five in November.

Bringing three daughters and two sons together has been an adventure. The girls were born and raised, prior to March 29, 1990 in a military environment. The guys were born around other family members and had their cousins nearby for the first several years. They moved to Mississippi for a time and then to the Columbia,

S.C. area where they completed high school and joined the Marines.

When anyone has a blended family, the natural parent usually needs to do the correcting until a relationship is established with the other parent. You can count on the children evaluating the way the new siblings are treated. If they see someone being allowed to do something they were not allowed to do in the past, they will make it known. They want the rules they have been made to follow to apply to their new siblings. This goes both ways. The best thing parents can do in a blended family is make decisions together, agree on what is expected, and not allow the children to divide them. The children need to know that their dad and mom stand as one in word and action.

It has taken time and consistency, but I now have a good relationship with Wes and Corey, and Sherry has a good relationship with Karena, Sabrina, and Christina.

My First Guide Dog—Kip

I used a cane for nine years before I decided to get a guide dog. Having used the cane for such a long time, I was concerned about getting around without it. Since I had no idea what a guide dog was capable of, I feared putting my trust in one.

After applying to Southeastern Guide Dogs located in Palmetto, FL, a person interviewed me to see how I would be using the dog. They wanted to know the structure of my family, the areas I would be walking in, whether there were sidewalks, or if I would be walking on the side of the road. They asked about public transportation, my work area, areas I frequented, and length of time I spent in one place. They also measured my stride and ability to correct the dog by jerking on the leash.

Once I arrived at the school, the trainer that was assigned to me did her own check of these areas. She then decided which dog would be best for me and my conditions. Later that same day, she brought me my guide dog, Kip. Kip and I spent time playing and bonding.

Each day the dog and I worked together, and we received obedience training, which I needed as much as Kip. We were taught how to groom the dog, how much to feed him, how to give him a bath, brush his teeth, and how to pick up after him when he went to "busy."

We discussed the various commands and were told not to use his name when telling him "heel, easy, no, or stay" because these are considered negative commands. While training together, if the dog didn't perform the way he was supposed to, I would have to correct him and let him try it again. Sometimes this required several repeats. We had to also be aware when the dog was becoming discouraged; he would drop his tail. The dog loved to wear the harness and got very excited when he saw us pick it up.

We started our training by walking around areas at the school. There were sidewalks and roads without sidewalks where we walked the edge of the road. After several steps, we would tell the dog, "stop, left," and after checking his alignment with the side of the road we commanded, "right, forward." We then went to downtown Bradenton and eventually to Tampa, FL for the day. During our visit in Tampa, after becoming confident in the dog's ability, I found myself slamming chest first into a parking meter. I hit it so hard that it left an imprint, and you could see where to put the nickel, the dime, and the quarter. This shortened my stride and dampened my pride. It didn't take long to regain my trust, but I learned the dog can get distracted and he didn't like walking over the steel grates on the sidewalk.

When I needed to cross a street, I commanded the dog to find the curb. I would then listen for the traffic in front of us to stop and for the traffic on our left or right to go. When they went, I would go with them giving the dog the commands, "forward, straight, and find the curb." When going into a store or building, I commanded the dog to find the door. When going up or down steps, I told Kip to find the steps and when he did, I would command him, "forward, up, or down." For escalators, I told him to find the escalator. I would then put my hand on the rail, and after determining the location of the steps, I commanded, "forward, on, and off." Kip was also trained to find elevators.

When he did, he would stand in front of the buttons so I could locate them. He was also taught to stop when a car pulled out in front of me, and how to get around an object that is blocking the sidewalk. This is done by locating the object such as a car and then commanding the dog, "left or right and around," making sure to go in the opposite direction of the street.

Upon completing the school, Kip and I flew from Tampa back to Columbia, SC. We were seated in the first row of seats behind the bulkhead. A man got on and sat down on the same row. He was a tad frustrated with the amount of time his family had given him to get to a funeral and he said, not noticing Kip, "You would think a dog died. I guess they think she is going to turn yellow, so they have to get her in the ground right away." He eventually noticed Kip and said rather shockingly "there's a dog on the plane." I laughed.

Kip was eighteen months old when I started training with him. He was a mix between a Golden and a Labrador Retriever. He was solid black with hair that glistened. Kip spent twelve months with a puppy raiser who exposed him to as many places and situations as she could. He received obedience training, and upon his return to the guide dog school, he received four to six months of additional instruction. I trained with him for twenty-six days. Kip and I were so attached that he watched my every move. If I was sitting down, he was beside me. When I got up, he got up. When I fed him, he waited to see if I was going to stay in the same room. If I walked out, he would eat his food quickly and then find me. At night he slept on the floor at the foot of my bed.

In April 2009, I found out Kip had lung cancer. He was treated intravenously and the cancer had all but gone. Once the number of intravenous treatments reached their limit, Kip was put on pills, which didn't keep the cancer under control. In August 2009, Kip was following me from the great room to the bedroom and collapsed in the hallway. I picked him up and put him in the car. We took him to the vet where he had received treatments and while there he perked up, but when we got him back home, he collapsed again and couldn't get up. I don't know of any decision I have ever made that was as tough as deciding to have Kip put down. The next morning Sherry, Kip, and I went to the office where the vet gave him an injection, and while part of my heart died with him, Kip passed into eternity. This dog gave me everything he had even until his last breath.

I returned to Southeastern Guide Dogs in September 2009 and trained with another guide dog named Senator.

He too is a mix of Golden and Lab, but he is multicolor with a lot of yellow and has, as I'm sure they all do, his own personality. When I sit down around Senator, he normally wants to roam the house to see what he can find. If I let him off the leash outside, he will take off to find other dogs in the neighborhood. However, he still gets excited when I pick up the harness, and he is always ready to go.

I think about all that God gave us, His only Begotten Son, who willingly died in our place and loved us even until His last breath here on this earth.

I don't know if there are animals in heaven, but I sure pray that Kip will be there when I arrive. I do know however, that my Savior lives and is seated at the right hand of the Father. He died so that we could live and see His glory and enjoy Him forever and ever. Is there more that He could have done? I think not.

CHAPTER

5

Is Anything Too Hard for God?

The day I flew out of Columbia
Metropolitan Airport on my way
to train with Senator, Sherry was
headed to her mother's house where
she was going to stay a week. On her
way there, the van we owned started
acting up. When she arrived at her
mom's, she had it checked and was
told that the engine was blown. She
called me at the school and told me
what had happened. We both began
praying. She prayed that God would
do something that only He could get
the credit for, and I was praying to

123

God about needing a new car. I said, "God, we need a new car but I don't have the money right now to buy one and I don't want to go in debt." God kept reminding me of Philippians 4:19 which says, **"and my God will supply all your needs according to His riches in glory in Christ Jesus."** I arrived back home on October 2, and my wife received a phone call from a couple at our church who told her that he, the husband, had something to share with us from God. I wasn't feeling well that day, so I called him the next day and told him I would love to hear what God has laid on his heart, but that we didn't have any way to get around right then. He began to tell me about the things God was doing in his life and then he said, "My wife and I believe God wants us to give you and Sherry our car." I initially said, "Brother, part of me wants to tell you 'don't do that.'" And he replied, "Part of me wants to say 'don't do that as well.'" I said, "Brother, before you change your mind...." (No, I didn't, I'm just joking.)

On October 5, he, his wife, and children brought us over a 2007 Toyota 4-Runner with less than 42,000 miles on it and signed it over. Can you say, "PRAISE THE LORD!?" Since that time, God has continued to bless us in ways that have left us speechless.

Ephesians 3:20-21 says, **"Now to Him who is able to do exceedingly abundantly above all that we ask or think, according to the power that works in us, to Him be glory in the church by Christ Jesus to all generations, forever and ever. Amen" (NKJV).**

Getting Through Tough Times

I was listening to the radio and heard Dr. Chuck Swindoll talk about what can help a person get through tough times. First he said, "You need to believe it can happen to you, whatever it is, you need to believe it can happen to you."

What I didn't realize was that I was going through a major depression where the serotonin in my brain had gotten to such a low level that I couldn't come out of it without help. It seemed that portions of my brain had actually shutdown, and I was unable to think beyond what I was doing. I would read the Bible, but all I felt was condemnation, and I had a constant bombardment of negative thoughts such as my family would be better off without me. If this has ever happened to you or is happening right now, I would like to help you understand the truth about these thoughts. I am speaking to you as a man who hit bottom and knows how tough it can be to get beyond what you are thinking.

Your family consists of you and the other members. If one of you dies, the family structure is fractured and will never be the same. You should not feel guilty for the thoughts you are having, as they are not you, they are part of depression. Please understand that it is not a weakness to ask for help. There is help available. You are not alone when struggling mentally and emotionally.

Perception is reality until overcome by truth. However, truth is only freeing when we accept it for ourselves. I couldn't think of anything that I had ever done that I considered to be right.

I have had people ask me why I

wanted to die. Even though I shot myself, I never thought about death. When I lost all hope, I didn't have anything else to hang on to. I would have to search the dictionary to briefly describe what it's like to be hopeless. I felt like a man who was already dead. My emotions were dull and lifeless. It was as if I was a container with nothing in it, an aircraft without engines, a bicycle without wheels, and/or a body without a soul and no way to get help.

When I think back on these things, I consider the utter torment it is to be separated from God and all that He is. Separated from love, joy, peace, kindness, goodness, faithfulness, gentleness, compassion, hope, mercy, forgiveness, grace, the Way, the Truth, the Life, the Word, and salvation.

When I was discharged from the Army in August 1990, I spent some time with my dad at his restaurant.

As we sat across the table one day, my dad said, "Joe, I'm sorry, I wish it could have been different." This was the first time in my life that I felt my dad was talking to me as if I really mattered. My visits prior to this time had always been short ones. I always felt like company and never like his son.

The memories I have of dad and mom being together are not good. Dad remarried but that marriage ended in divorce as well. I recall dad driving a long distance truck for Mayflower and then opening a bar, but I'm not sure how long he operated it. He met a lady and moved to Florida for a time. They eventually got married. He was a carpenter by trade, but served as a mess sergeant while in the Army. His last venture was to open a restaurant that operated twenty-four hours a day. He ran that for several years before he died in mid-1991.

During one of our conversations, dad told me that he had once struggled with thoughts of suicide himself. He said there was a time when he had a gun to his head and a friend stopped him from pulling the trigger. I also learned that my mom had struggled with depression in her past.

In 1994 my wife and I had a thirteen-year-old daughter admitted to long-term hospitalization in Atlanta, GA for alcohol and drug abuse. We thank God that three and a half months later she came out a different person.

When Ethel moved back to Sumter, S.C., she started working at a bar. Her drinking got worse, and I received a phone call on April 24, 2003 and was told by the man she had married that she had been in a single car accident and was killed. Her car crossed the left lane and went into a ditch hitting an embankment. A blood alcohol test was performed, and her blood alcohol level was .404.

I believe we can learn from others and not follow the same path they followed if we are willing to heed what we know they have done and the consequences they suffered. When we see someone burn their hand on a stove, we don't put our hand on it saying, "I can't believe that burned you." When we hear about someone getting in a wreck and being charged with DUI, we don't say, "I wish I would have had that happen to me." Why? Because we don't normally want things to happen to us that bring pain or hinder us in any way. However, we will do the same things we know others have done and not even give a second thought about what happened to them or that it could happen to us.

I want you to hang on to this statement, "When I do what others do, I will, at some point, suffer the same or similar consequences they suffered."

Please read the following and ask yourself, "Could I put my name in one or more of these examples?"

Example 1: When I, (name), consume alcohol and drive, I will at some point be charged with a DUI; get in a wreck; take the life of another human being; or lose my own life.

Example 2: When I, (name), have an extramarital affair, I will at some point see my wife and children's hearts crushed, my family dissolved, and others hurt.

Example 3: When I, (name), lie, cheat, steal, manipulate, or use people for personal reasons, I will at some point be found out and suffer the loss of a good name, friendships, family, finances, and possibly my freedom.

Example 4: When I, (name),

have sexual relationships outside of marriage, I will at some point be faced with pregnancy, being a single parent, be encouraged to get an abortion, have overwhelming thoughts of being a mother having to grow up too soon, and wondering what my parents will say and do.

Example 5: When I, (name), get involved with drugs, I will at some point be charged with possession, locked up, lose my car, have an overdose, die from a heart attack, or as a friend did, walk out in front of an eighteen wheeler.

The situations above are real. They have happened to many and can happen to many more. I pray you won't be one of them.

I believe the reason we are willing to do what others have done without thought of consequences, is because we are willing to get involved in those things that bring pleasure before they bring pain. Please allow me to say that again. I believe the reason we do what others have done, without thought of consequences, is because we are willing to get involved in those things that bring pleasure before they bring pain.

In Galatians 6:7 we read, **"Be not deceived; God is not mocked: for whatsoever a man soweth, that shall he also reap" (KJV).**

This is not God saying, "I'm just waiting for you to do something wrong so I can punish you." It is His love for us that moves Him to warn us that many of our actions bring negative consequences to us as well as others.

Whatever it is, you need to believe it can happen to you.

Second, you need someone who is willing to put their arm around you when the time is right and tell you it's time to move on. I learned when it seemed I had lost practically everything that what really mattered was there all the time. I don't believe there is anything we can have that's worth losing a relationship with God or our family. Please be honest with yourself and consider what really matters to you.

I have had numerous people come in and out of my life that in one way or another have helped me move on. This is not to say I have never slipped back. There have been many times the way was slippery and uncertain.

Lieutenant Colonel Dennis and Connie Duffey have been faithful friends both in and out of the Army. They are the kind of friends that I knew I could count on no matter what the situation. Chief Warrant Officer Erv and Mary Shaw lived next door to us at Fort Bragg, N.C. Erv and I were in the same unit there as well as in Korea. We have stayed in contact and have been to see each other several times since. I arrived home in Virginia to find Earl Blackmon waiting to see me. He had brought talking clocks, watches, and other items to assist me. Roger Brock and Ken and Beverly Dunlap, along with their families, helped the girls and me tremendously. They included me in their plans and helped with everyday tasks and kept the yard manicured.

I went with Ken and Beverly to Lakewood Camp Grounds. They had a camper we stayed in. Ken and Beverly were always looking out for me. Ken and I were running around the campground, using my cane to connect with each other. A van pulled around us and then stopped. Ken was able to get to the side, but I hit the back of the van. After peeling me off the van, Ken asked, "Why don't you watch where you are going?"

I crawled in bed one evening to find that Ken and Beverly had put popcorn between my sheets. They said it was in case I got hungry during the night. I got up to use the restroom and found that Ken had pulled the drawers out for me to run into. Occasionally, I would treat them with the same respect. I was eating a banana and when I finished, I called Ken's name. When he answered, I got a bull's eye in his face with my banana peel. I accidentally, on purpose, knocked his drink over on him while at McDonalds. I asked Beverly to help me put mustard on my sandwich and felt her run it up my arm. We would occasionally go to yard sales. One day when it was raining, we stopped at a sale that was being displayed in a person's garage. Ken didn't want to get out because of the rain. I told him he was a wimp. He then decided that he would go with me. The garage was on the left side of the house. Ken walked me to the right end of the house, put me under the eve where the rain was pouring off, and then walked me to the other end. When I arrived at the garage, I was soaked.

Roger Brock often treated me with the same dignity. Roger allowed me to drive his car on a rural road. I had to keep smacking his hand as he kept trying to grab the steering wheel.

Ken drove us to Florida and went with me, my daughter Christina, and her friend Catherine, on a graduation cruise. We had a great time. Ken and I were running around the deck when a lady running in the opposite direction collided with me. Fortunately, we didn't hit heads. We bounced off each other and Ken said, "I think you hurt her." We stopped her and apologized. She told us about growing up with three brothers and that she was fine.

There was a period of time that I was stuck. I had a hard time making everyday decisions and had to start asking myself, "What would any reasonable person do?" After learning how to evaluate my thinking with my feelings and my actions, I tried to ensure I had the right balance in these areas.

Sherry is a great wife, friend, mom, grandmother, and encourager. She loves the Lord and helps me stay focused on the truth of God's Word. We have struggled together with various situations with our children, and thanks to her, we have been able to raise two grandchildren for most of their lives. Sherry brought the addition of two sons, Wesley and Corey. Having spent the time I did in the Army, I always wanted to have a few good men, Marines, I could help. I don't have them convinced that they made the wrong choice, but I'm working on it.

My grandson and I would walk down the street, through the woods, across the railroad tracks, and go to Dollar General. When we first started, I was able to put my hand on top of his head as he led me. Now he's about an inch shorter than I am. There were at least four occasions that people came up to us and told him what a wonderful thing it was to see him, a child, helping his granddad. They expressed that it was very uncommon now, and they would hand him money to spend in the store. I also remember on one occasion a lady was standing at the corner of the building, and when we walked by, she stopped us to encourage him for what he was doing.

After Sherry and I were married, she shared a note with me that she had written before we ever started dating. God revealed to her that I was going to be her husband.

For the past few years, I have assisted the Missions Pastor of Christian Life Church. We have endeavored to train and encourage our church family and others to prepare for unexpected emergency situations. Thankfully, there are others in the church that were already preparing and joined with us to help.

In April 2014, Sherry and I were staying with mom in the hospital when she passed from this life to her eternal home. She had been diagnosed with cancer. During the months prior to hospitalization, my oldest brother, my sister, and their spouses were taking care of her. Mom had been seeing someone in her room. She kept asking,

"Who is that man?"

The morning she passed away, she told Sherry that she saw her dad. Sherry asked her if he looked good. Mom said he looked young. Shortly after this it seemed mom saw something that really excited her, and in her last breath, she said, "Praise the Lord."

My brothers, sister, and I along with our families were very close to our mom and had the privilege of having her with us for almost eighty-nine years. We need other people. We were never meant to walk alone. "Walking in the dark with a friend is better than walking alone in the light." ~ Helen Keller (Helen was blind from birth.)

Third, Dr. Swindoll said, you need to know Jesus Christ as your personal Savior. John 3:16-17 says, **"For God** so loved the world, that He gave His only begotten Son, that whoever believes in Him shall not perish, but have eternal life. For God did not send the Son into the world to judge the world, but that the world might be saved through Him."

As I sat in the pastor's home that morning, he shared with me what it says in Romans 3:23, **"For all have sinned and fall short of the glory of God" (NKJV).** And he told me someone had to pay for those sins, because it says in Romans 6:23, **"For the wages of sin is death, but the gift of God is eternal life in Christ Jesus our Lord" (NKJV).**

He said, "Joe, if you realize that you are a sinner and you believe that Christ died for your sins, and you are willing to accept the free gift He has made available to you, then all you have to do is what it says in Romans 10:13, **'for whosoever shall call upon the name of the Lord shall be saved'"** **(KJV).** He is the Way, the Truth, and the Life as we are told in John 14:6; and no man comes unto the Father but through Him. He is not one way, but THE WAY and He is waiting for you.

We have discussed three of the four things that Dr. Swindoll said could help someone to get through tough times. He said first, you need to believe it can happen to you, whatever it is, you need to believe it can happen to you. Second, you need someone who is willing to put their arm around you, when the time is right, and tell you it's time to move on. Third, you need to know Jesus Christ as your personal Savior. And lastly, you need to have unwavering faith.

One thing I realize now is that God's Word is true whether I believe it or not—my unbelief does not change God's faithfulness. God is perfectly holy; He cannot lie. His Word tells us "though every man be a liar, he remains true."

When God says He will never leave us nor forsake us, that's exactly what He means. When we can't count on our best friend, we can count on God. When we can't count on our boss, we can count on God. When we can't count on ourselves, we can count on God. And when we can't count on what we feel, hear, or even see, we can count on God.

When we lose all hope, we need only remember that God is the God of all hope. That He is the one who holds all power in heaven and earth. That He is our mediator and our intercessor—we are cleansed by His blood and that He takes pleasure in having a relationship with us.

The Bible tells us that God is the author and finisher of our faith. We are told in Romans 10:17 that **"faith comes from hearing, and hearing by the word of God."** (Remember God and His Word are one in the same.) We see this in John 1:1 where we are told, **"In the beginning was the Word, and the Word was with God, and the Word was God."** Then in John 1:14 we see that the Word, Jesus Christ, became flesh and dwelt among us. So what this means to me is that everything that Jesus Christ said and did while here on this earth was a demonstration of the Word of God in living, breathing form.

With this in mind, we can be assured that the Word of God, Christ Jesus, is as close to us today as He was when He lived in the flesh. He is the same yesterday, today, and forever.

"Our Creator is the same and never changes despite the names given Him by people here as well as in all parts of the world. Even if we gave Him no name at all, He would still be there, within us, waiting to give us good on this earth."
~ George Washington Carver

II Corinthians 5:7 says, **"for we walk by faith, not by sight."** This requires obedience. As a blind man, I have had to learn to use a cane and to trust my guide dog. When I decide to get around without the use of either, I have fallen into pools, walked into walls, cabinets, doors, people, and recently I stepped out of the back of a Budget truck, missing the ramp and broke two ribs. I am meant to use what is available to me. As a Christian, my cane is the Bible and obedience to His Word is my guide dog.

We are given a word to stand on in II Timothy 2:13 which says, **"If we are faithless, He remains faithful, for He cannot deny Himself."**

Additionally, we are encouraged in Isaiah 41:10, **"Fear not, for I am with you; be not dismayed, for I am your God, I will strengthen you. Yes I will help you, I will uphold you with My righteous right hand"** (NKJV).

Then in II Peter 1:3 we read, **"Seeing that His divine power has granted to us everything pertaining to life and godliness, through the**

true knowledge of Him who called us by His own glory and excellence." This covers it all!

GOD IS HIS WORD!

I encourage you to put your trust in Him.

Summary

I want to finish this book with a poem the Lord gave me in 1991. I named it, "Thank You, Lord" and tried for several months to write it, but I couldn't come up with the words. I was scheduled to share at a church on Thanksgiving weekend, when the day before God gave me this poem. I wanted to express my gratitude to God, my family, and those who stood with me. I also wanted to express how at times I feel less than a man, how my friends were all seemingly gone, and how God never forsook me, and the hope that I still have.

THANK YOU, LORD

*For Your saving grace and strength
for whatever I may face.*

*For hearing me in my time of need
and showing me of Your Word I
must heed.*

*For giving me a new start and
opening the eyes of my heart.*

*For when I feared of being less than
a man, You have shown me O Lord
that when I can't You can.*

*For when my friends had all
seemingly gone, You O Lord did not
leave me alone.*

*For a wife who is strong and true,
one who comforts, encourages, and
believes in me too.*

*For our children and grandchildren
too what they are and have yet to be
in You.*

*For the paths I cross each day and
that by Your grace my life may show
Your way.*

*For the sky I cannot see and the sky
You have given to me.*

*For the flowers I cannot smell and
the flowers of which to others I may
tell.*

*For making and molding me, loving
and holding me.*

*For always leading and guiding,
protecting and providing
and
Thank You Lord*

*For teaching me to see from within
and knowing that when this short
life is over, I will see again.*

APPENDICES

Appendix A

Renewing Your Mind By Focusing On Truth

"Within the covers of the Bible are the answers to all the problems men face."
~ President Ronald Reagan

The Scriptures noted below bring comfort and encouragement to me during dark times.

Philippians 4:6-7: Be anxious for nothing, but in everything by prayer and supplication with thanksgiving let your requests be made known to God. And the peace of God, which surpasses all comprehension, will guard your hearts and your minds in Christ Jesus.

Philippians 4:8: Finally, brethren, whatever things are true, whatever things are noble, whatever things are just, whatever things are pure, whatever things are lovely, whatever things are of good report, if there is any virtue and if there is anything praiseworthy—meditate on these things (NKJV).

Romans 12:2: And do not be conformed to this world, but be transformed by the renewing of your mind....

Proverbs 3:5-6: Trust in the Lord with all your heart, and lean

not on your own understanding;
in all your ways acknowledge Him,
and He shall direct your paths
(NKJV).

Isaiah 40:8: The grass
withers, the flower fades, but the
word of our God stands forever
(NKJV).

Psalm 32:8: I will instruct
you and teach you in the way you
should go. I will guide you with
My eye (NKJV).

Psalm 119:105: Your word
is a lamp to my feet and a light to
my path.

Romans 8:28: And we know
all things work together for good
to those who love God, to those
who are the called according to

His purpose (NKJV).

Psalm 32:7: You are my hiding place; You shall preserve me from trouble; You shall surround me with songs of deliverance (NKJV).

Psalm 37:4: Delight yourself also in the Lord, and He shall give you the desires of your heart (NKJV).

Romans 8:24-25: For we were saved in this hope, but hope that is seen is not hope, for why does one still hope for what he sees? But if we hope for what we do not see, we eagerly wait for it with perseverance (NKJV).

John 3:16-17: For God so loved the world that He gave His

only begotten Son, that whoever believes in Him shall not perish, but have everlasting life. For God did not send His Son into the world to condemn the world, but that the world through Him might be saved (NKJV).

I John 1:9: If we confess our sins, He is faithful and just to forgive us our sins and to cleanse us from all unrighteousness (NKJV).

I John 3:20: For if our heart condemns us, God is greater than our heart, and knows all things (NKJV).

Romans 8:1: There is therefore now no condemnation for those who are in Christ Jesus, who do not walk according to the flesh, but according to the Spirit (NKJV).

Romans 8:32-34: He who did not spare His own Son, but delivered Him up for us all, how shall He not with Him also freely give us all things? Who will bring a charge against God's elect? It is God who justifies. Who is he who condemns? It is Christ who died, and furthermore is also risen, who is even at the right hand of God, who also makes intercession for us (NKJV).

Psalm 46:1: God is our refuge and strength, a very present help in trouble (NKJV).

II Timothy 2:13: If we are faithless, He remains faithful; He cannot deny Himself (NKJV).

Jeremiah 1:12: Then the Lord said to me, "You have seen well (I am alert and active, watching over my Word to perform it), **for I am ready to perform My word**" **(NKJV).**

Romans 10:17: So then faith comes by hearing, and hearing by the word of God (NKJV).

II Corinthians 5:7: For we walk by faith, not by sight.

Isaiah 54:17: No weapon that is formed against you shall prosper, and every tongue that accuses you in judgment you shall condemn.

Psalm 34:18-19: The Lord is near to the brokenhearted and

saves those who are crushed in spirit. Many are the afflictions of the righteous, but the Lord delivers him out of them all.

Isaiah 40:31: But those who wait on the Lord shall renew their strength; they shall mount up with wings like eagles, they shall run and not be weary, they shall walk and not faint (NKJV).

Psalm 46:10: Be still, and know that I am God (NKJV).

Isaiah 41:10: Fear not for I am with you; be not dismayed, for I am your God. I will strengthen you, yes, I will help you. I will uphold you with My righteous right hand (NKJV).

I John 4:18: There is no fear

in love; but perfect love cast out fear.

Romans 5:8: But God demonstrates His own love toward us, in that while we were yet sinners, Christ died for us.

John 15:13: Greater love has no one than this, that one lay down his life for his friends.

Philippians 4:13: I can do all things through Him who strengthens me.

Philippians 4:19: And my God shall supply all your needs according to His riches in glory in Christ Jesus.

Jeremiah 29:11: For I know the thoughts that I think toward

APPENDIX B

Depression Symptoms and Warning Signs
How to Recognize Depression Symptoms and Get Effective Help

The normal ups and downs of life mean that everyone feels sad or has "the blues" from time to time. But if emptiness and despair have taken hold of your life and won't go away, you may have depression. Depression makes it tough to function and enjoy life like you once did. Just getting through the day can be overwhelming. But no matter how hopeless you feel, you can get better. Understanding the signs, symptoms, causes, and treatment of depression is the first step to overcoming the problem.

What is depression?

Sadness or downswings in mood are normal reactions to life's struggles, setbacks, and disappointments. Many people use the word "depression" to explain these kinds of feelings, but depression is much more than just sadness.

Some people describe depression as "living in a black hole" or having a feeling of impending doom. However, some depressed people don't feel sad at all-they may feel lifeless, empty, and apathetic, or men in particular may even feel angry, aggressive, and restless.

Whatever the symptoms, depression is different from normal sadness in that it engulfs your day-to-day life, interfering with your ability to work, study, eat, sleep, and have fun. The feelings of helplessness, hopelessness, and worthlessness are intense and unrelenting, with little, if any, relief.

Are you depressed?

If you identify with several of the following signs and symptoms, and they just won't go away, you may be suffering from clinical depression:

- you can't sleep or you sleep too much
- you can't concentrate or find that previously easy tasks are now difficult
- you feel hopeless and helpless
- you can't control your negative thoughts, no matter how much you try
- you have lost your appetite or you can't stop eating
- you are much more irritable, short-tempered, or aggressive than usual
- you're consuming more alcohol

than normal or engaging in other reckless behavior
* you have thoughts that life is not worth living (seek help *immediately* if this is the case)

What are the signs and symptoms of depression?

Depression varies from person to person, but there are some common signs and symptoms. It's important to remember that these symptoms can be part of life's normal lows. But the more symptoms you have, the stronger they are, and the longer they've lasted-the more likely it is that you're dealing with depression. When these symptoms are overwhelming and disabling, that's when it's time to seek help.

Signs and symptoms of depression include:

Feelings of helplessness and hopelessness. A bleak outlook-nothing will ever get better and there's nothing you can do to improve your situation.

Loss of interest in daily activities. No interest in former hobbies, pastimes, social activities, or sex. You've lost your ability to feel joy and pleasure.

Appetite or weight changes. Significant weight loss or weight gain-a change of more than 5% of body weight in a month.

Sleep changes. Either insomnia, especially waking in the early hours of the morning, or oversleeping (also known as hypersomnia).

Anger or irritability. Feeling agitated, restless, or even violent. Your tolerance level is low, your temper short, and everything and everyone gets on your nerves.

Loss of energy. Feeling fatigued, sluggish, and physically drained. Your whole body may feel heavy, and even small tasks are exhausting or take longer to complete.

Self-loathing. Strong feelings of worthlessness or guilt. You harshly criticize yourself for perceived faults and mistakes.

Reckless behavior. You engage in escapist behavior such as substance abuse, compulsive gambling, reckless driving, or dangerous sports.

Concentration problems. Trouble focusing, making decisions, or remembering things.

Unexplained aches and pains. An

increase in physical complaints such as headaches, back pain, aching muscles, and stomach pain.

Depression and Suicide Risk

Depression is a major risk factor for suicide. The deep despair and hopelessness that goes along with depression can make suicide feel like the only way to escape the pain. If you have a loved one with depression, take any suicidal talk or behavior seriously and learn to recognize the warning signs.

3Warning signs of suicide include:
- Talking about killing or harming one's self
- Expressing strong feelings of hopelessness or being trapped
- An unusual preoccupation with death or dying

- Acting recklessly, as if they have a death wish (e.g. speeding through red lights)
- Calling or visiting people to say goodbye
- Getting affairs in order (giving away prized possessions, tying up loose ends)
- Saying things like "Everyone would be better off without me" or "I want out"
- A sudden switch from being extremely depressed to acting calm and happy

If You Are Feeling Suicidal...

When you're feeling extremely depressed or suicidal, your problems don't seem temporary—they seem overwhelming and permanent. But with time, you will feel better, especially if you reach out for help.

If you are feeling suicidal, know that there are many people who want to support you during this difficult time, so please reach out for help!

Read <u>Suicide Help</u> or call **1-800-273-TALK** in the U.S. or visit <u>IASP</u> or <u>Suicide.org</u> to find a helpline in your country.

If Someone You Love is Suicidal...

If you think a friend or family member is considering suicide, express your concern and seek professional help immediately. Talking openly about suicidal thoughts and feelings can save a life! **Read** <u>Suicide Prevention</u>.

The Different Faces of Depression

Depression often looks different in men and women, and in young people and older adults. An awareness of these differences helps ensure that the problem is recognized and treated.

Depression in Men

Depression is a loaded word in our culture. Many associate it, however wrongly, with a sign of weakness and excessive emotion. This is especially true with men. Depressed men are less likely than women to acknowledge feelings of self-loathing and hopelessness. Instead, they tend to complain about fatigue, irritability, sleep problems, and loss of interest in work and hobbies. Other signs and symptoms of depression in men include anger, aggression, violence, reckless behavior, and substance abuse. Even though depression rates for women are twice as high as those in men, men are a higher suicide risk, especially older men. Learn more.

Depression in women

Rates of depression in women are twice as high as they are in men. This is due in part to hormonal factors, particularly when it comes to premenstrual syndrome (PMS), premenstrual dysphonic disorder (PMDD), postpartum depression, and perimenopausal depression. As for signs and symptoms, women are more likely than men to experience pronounced feelings of guilt, sleep excessively, overeat, and gain weight. Women are also more likely to suffer from seasonal affective disorder. Learn more.

Depression in Teens

While some depressed teens appear sad, others do not. In fact, irritability-rather than depression-is frequently the predominant symptom in depressed adolescents and teens.

A depressed teenager may be hostile, grumpy, or easily lose his or her temper. Unexplained aches and pains are also common symptoms of depression in young people.

Left untreated, teen depression can lead to problems at home and school, drug abuse, self-loathing-even irreversible tragedy such as homicidal violence or suicide. But with help, teenage depression is highly treatable. Learn more.

Depression in Older Adults

The difficult changes that many older adults face-such as bereavement, loss of independence, and health problems-can lead to depression, especially in those without a strong support system. However, depression is not a normal part of aging. Older adults tend to complain more about the physical rather than the emotional signs and symptoms of depression, and so the problem often goes unrecognized. Depression in older adults is associated with poor health, a high mortality rate, and an increased risk of suicide, so diagnosis and treatment are extremely important. Learn more.

Postpartum Depression

Many new mothers suffer from some fleeting form of the "baby blues." Postpartum depression, in contrast, is a longer lasting and more serious depression triggered, in part, by hormonal changes associated with having a baby. Postpartum depression usually develops soon after delivery, but any depression that occurs within six months of childbirth may be postpartum depression.

What are the Types of Depression?

Depression comes in many shapes and forms. The different types of depression have unique symptoms, causes, and effects. Knowing what type of depression you have can help you manage your symptoms and get the most effective treatment.

Major Depression

Major depression is characterized by the inability to enjoy life and experience pleasure. The symptoms are constant, ranging from moderate to severe. Left untreated, major depression typically lasts for about six months. Some people experience just a single depressive episode in their lifetime, but more commonly, major depression is a recurring disorder. However, there are many things you can do to support your mood and reduce the risk of recurrence.

Dysthymia (recurrent, mild depression)

Dysthymia is a type of chronic "low-grade" depression. More days than not, you feel mildly or moderately depressed, although you may have brief periods of normal mood. The symptoms of dysthymia are not as strong as the symptoms of major depression, but they last a long time (at least two years). These chronic symptoms make it very difficult to live life to the fullest or to remember better times. Some people also experience major depressive episodes on top of dysthymia, a condition known as "double depression." If you suffer from dysthymia, you may feel like you've always been depressed. Or you may think that your continuous low mood is "just the way you are." However, dysthymia can be treated, even if your symptoms have gone unrecognized or untreated for years.

Bipolar Disorder: When Depression is Just One Side of the Coin

Bipolar disorder, also known as manic depression, is characterized by cycling mood changes. Episodes of depression alternate with *manic episodes*, which can include impulsive behavior, hyperactivity, rapid speech, and little to no sleep. Typically, the switch from one mood extreme to the other is gradual, with each manic or depressive episode lasting for at least several weeks. When depressed, a person with bipolar disorder exhibits the usual symptoms of major depression. However, the treatments for bipolar depression are very different. In fact, antidepressants can make bipolar depression worse.

Seasonal affective disorder: When winter brings the blues

Many people feel sad when summer

wanes, but some actually develop depression with the season's change. Known as seasonal affective disorder (SAD), this form of depression affects about 1% to 2% of the population, particularly women and young people. SAD seems to be triggered by more limited exposure to daylight; typically it comes on during the fall or winter months and subsides in the spring.

To combat SAD, doctors suggest exercise, particularly outdoor activities during daylight hours. Exposing yourself to bright artificial light may also help. Light therapy, also called phototherapy, usually involves sitting close to a special light source that is far more intense than normal indoor light for 30 minutes every morning. The light must enter through your eyes to be effective; skin exposure has not been proven to work. Some people feel better after only one light treatment, but most people require at least a few days of treatment, and some need several weeks. You can buy boxes that emit the proper light intensity (10,000 lux) with a minimal amount of ultraviolet light without a prescription, but it is best to work with a professional who can monitor your response.

There are few side effects to light therapy, but you should be aware of the following potential problems:

- Mild anxiety, jitteriness, headaches, early awakening, or eyestrain can occur.
- There is evidence that light therapy can trigger a manic episode in people who are vulnerable.
- While there is no proof that light therapy can aggravate an

eye problem, you should still discuss any eye disease with your doctor before starting light therapy. Likewise, since rashes can result, let your doctor know about any skin conditions.

- Some drugs or herbs (for example, St. John's Wort) can make you sensitive to light.

Adapted with permission from _Understanding Depression_, a special health report published by Harvard Health Publications.

Depression Causes and Risk Factors

Some illnesses have a specific medical cause, making treatment straightforward. If you have Type-1 diabetes, you take insulin. If you have appendicitis, you have surgery. Depression, however, is more complicated. Depression is not just the result of a chemical imbalance in the brain, and it's not simply cured with medication. Experts believe that depression is caused by a combination of biological, psychological, and social factors. In other words, your lifestyle choices, relationships, and coping skills matter just as much—if not more so—than genetics. However, certain risk factors make you more vulnerable to depression.

Causes and Risk Factors for Depression

- Loneliness
- Lack of social support
- Recent stressful life experiences
- Family history of depression
- Marital or relationship problems
- Financial strain
- Early childhood trauma or abuse
- Alcohol or drug abuse

- Unemployment or underemployment
- Health problems or chronic pain

The Cause of Your Depression Helps Determine the Treatment

Understanding the underlying cause of your depression may help you overcome the problem. For example, if you are depressed because of a dead end job, the best treatment might be finding a more satisfying career, not taking an antidepressant. If you are new to an area and feeling lonely and sad, finding new friends at work or through a hobby will probably give you more of a mood boost than going to therapy. In such cases, the depression is remedied by changing the situation.

The Road to Depression Recovery

Just as the symptoms and causes of

depression are different in different people, so are the ways to feel better. What works for one person might not work for another, and no one treatment is appropriate in all cases. If you recognize the signs of depression in yourself or a loved one, take some time to explore the many treatment options. In most cases, the best approach involves a combination of social support, lifestyle changes, emotional skills building, and professional help.

Ask for Help and Support

If even the thought of tackling your depression seems overwhelming, don't panic. Feeling helpless and hopeless is a symptom of depression- not the reality of your situation. It does *not* mean that you're weak or you can't change! The key to depression recovery is to start small and *ask for help.* The simple act of talking to someone face to face about how you feel can be an enormous help. The person you talk to doesn't have to be able to fix you; he or she just needs to be a good listener.

Having a strong support system will speed your recovery. Isolation fuels depression, so reach out to others, even if you feel like being alone or don't want to feel like a burden to others. The truth is that most people will be happy that you chose to confide in them; they'll be flattered that you trust them enough to open up. So, let your family and friends know what you're going through and how they can support you.

Make Healthy Lifestyle Changes

Lifestyle changes are not always easy to make, but they can have a big impact on depression. Lifestyle changes that can be very effective include:

- Cultivating supportive relationships
- Getting regular exercise and sleep
- Eating healthfully to naturally boost mood
- Managing stress
- Practicing relaxation techniques
- Challenging negative thought patterns

Build Emotional Skills

Many people lack the skills needed to manage stress and balance emotions. Building emotional skills can give you the ability to cope and bounce back from adversity, trauma, and loss. In other words, learning how to recognize and express your emotions can make you more resilient.

Seek Professional Help

If support from family and friends, positive lifestyle changes, and emotional skills building aren't enough, seek help from a mental health professional. There are many effective treatments for depression, including therapy, medication, and alternative treatments. Learning about your options will help you decide what measures are most likely to work best for your particular situation and needs.

Are Antidepressants Right for You?

Medication can help relieve the symptoms of depression in some people, but they aren't a cure and they come with drawbacks of their own. Learning the facts about antidepressants and weighing the benefits against the risks can help you make an informed and personal decision about whether medication is right for you.

Effective treatment for depression often includes some form of therapy. Therapy gives you tools to treat depression from a variety of angles. Also, what you learn in therapy gives you skills and insight to prevent depression from coming back.

Some types of therapy teach you practical techniques on how to reframe negative thinking and employ behavioral skills in combating depression. Therapy can also help you work through the root of your depression, helping you understand why you feel a certain way, what your triggers are for depression, and what you can do to stay healthy.

More Help for Depression
Depression in Older Adults: Recognize the Signs and Find Treatment that Works

Parent's Guide to Teen Depression: Learn the Signs and How You Can Help Your Teen

Teenager's Guide to Depression: Learn Tips and Tools for Helping Yourself or a Friend

Depression in Men: Why It's Hard to Recognize and What Helps

Depression in Women: Causes, Symptoms, Treatment, and Self-Help

Dealing with Depression: Self-Help and Coping Tips to Overcome Depression

Helping a Depressed Person: How to Reach Out and Help Someone While Taking Care of Yourself

Postpartum Depression: Symptoms, Treatment, and Support for New Mothers

Bipolar Disorder Signs and Symptoms: Recognizing Mania, Hypomania and Bipolar Depression

Antidepressant Medication:

What You Need to Know About Medications for Depression Depression Treatment: Therapy, Medication, and Lifestyle Changes That Can Help Depression

Resources and References
Signs and Symptoms of Depression
Signs and Symptoms of Mood Disorders —Lists the common signs and symptoms of depression and bipolar disorder. (Depression and Bipolar Support Alliance)
Real Stories of Depression —Read personal stories of depression, review the signs and symptoms, and learn how to get help. (National Institute of Mental Health)
What Does Depression Feel Like? — Provides a list of signs and symptoms and ways you might feel if you're depressed. (Wings of Madness)

When Depression Hurts —Article
on the painful physical symptoms of
depression, including what causes
them and how treatment can help.
(Psychology Today)
Male Depression: Don't Ignore
the Symptoms —Learn about the
distinct symptoms of depression in
men and the dangers of leaving them
untreated. (Mayo Clinic)

Types of Depression
The Different Faces of Depression
—Discussion of the different
subtypes of depression, including
atypical depression, melancholic
depression, and psychotic depression.
(Psychology Today)
Atypical Depression: What's in a
Name? —Article on the symptoms,
diagnosis, and treatment of atypical
depression. (American Psychiatric
Association)

—In-depth look at the causes, effects, and treatment of dysthymic disorder. (Harvard Health Publications)
Seasonal Affective Disorder: Winter Depression —Guide to seasonal affective disorder and its symptoms, causes, and treatment. (Northern County Psychiatric Associates)

Depression Causes and Risk Factors

What Causes Depression? Page 1 & Page 2 —Learn about the many potential causes of depression, including genes, temperament, stressful life events, and medical issues. (Harvard Health Publications)
Depression and Other Illnesses —An overview of the mental and physical illnesses that often co-exist with depression, and how this impacts treatment. (Depression and Bipolar

Support Alliance)
Co-occurring Disorders and Depression
—How medical disorders can affect
depression and vice versa. (Mental
Health America)
*Authors: Melinda Smith, M.A., Joanna
Saisan, M.S.W., and Jeanne Segal, Ph.D.
Last updated: April 2015.*

Depression in Women
Helping a Depressed Person
Borderline Personality Disorder

©Helpguide.org. All rights reserved.
This reprint is for information
only and NOT a substitute for
professional diagnosis and treatment.
Helpguide.org is an ad-free nonprofit resource for supporting better
mental health and lifestyle choices for
adults and children.

USED WITH PERMISSION

Appendix C

Suicide Help
Dealing with Suicidal Thoughts and Feelings

In This Article

You're not alone; many of us have had suicidal thoughts at some point in our lives. Feeling suicidal is not a character defect, and it doesn't mean that you are crazy, or weak, or flawed. It only means that you have more pain than you can cope with right now. This pain seems overwhelming and permanent at the moment. But with time and support, you can overcome your problems and the pain and suicidal feelings will pass.

Coping with suicidal thoughts: the first steps.

Step #1: Promise not to do anything right now.

Even though you're in a lot of pain right now, give yourself some distance between thoughts and action. Make a promise to yourself: "I will wait 24 hours and won't do anything drastic during that time." Or, wait a week.

Thoughts and actions are two different things-your suicidal thoughts do not have to become a reality. There is no deadline, no one pushing you to act on these thoughts immediately. Wait. Wait and put some distance between your suicidal thoughts and suicidal action.

Step #2: Avoid drugs and alcohol
Suicidal thoughts can become even stronger if you have taken drugs or alcohol. It is important to not use nonprescription drugs or alcohol when you feel hopeless or are thinking about suicide.

Step #3: Make your home safe

Remove things you could use to hurt yourself, such as pills, knives, razors, or firearms. If you are unable to do so, go to a place where you can feel safe. If you are thinking of taking an overdose, give your medicines to someone who can return them to you one day at a time as you need them.

Step #4: Take hope-people DO get through this

Even people who feel as badly as you are feeling now manage to survive these feelings. Take hope in this. There is a very good chance that you are going to live through these feelings, no matter how much self-loathing, hopelessness, or isolation you are currently experiencing. Just give yourself the time needed and don't try to go it alone.

Step #5: Don't keep these suicidal

feelings to yourself

Many of us have found that the first step to coping with suicidal thoughts and feelings is to share them with someone we trust. It may be a friend, a therapist, a member of the clergy, a teacher, a family doctor, a coach, or an experienced counselor at the end of a helpline. Find someone you trust and let them know how bad things are. Don't let fear, shame, or embarrassment prevent you from seeking help. Just talking about how you got to this point in your life can release a lot of the pressure that's building up and help you find a way to cope.

If you're feeling suicidal right now, please call for help! Call 1-800-273-TALK in the U.S. or visit <u>IASP</u> to find a helpline in your country. Or talk to someone you trust and let them know how bad things are.

Why do I feel this way?

Many kinds of emotional pain can lead to thoughts of suicide. The reasons for this pain are unique to each one of us, and our ability to cope with the pain differs from person to person. Don't listen to anyone who tells you, "That's not enough to be suicidal about." We are all different. What might be bearable to one person may not be bearable to you. There are, however, some common factors that may lead us to experience suicidal thoughts and feelings.

Feeling suicidal is often associated with problems that can be treated

Loss, depression, anxiety disorders, medical conditions, drug and alcohol dependency, financial, legal or school problems, and other life difficulties can all create profound emotional distress. They also interfere with our ability to problem solve. Even if you can't see it now, there are nearly always other solutions for these problems.

Mental health conditions such as depression , anxiety, and bipolar disorder are all treatable with changes in lifestyle, therapy, and medication. Most people who seek help for their problems and make constructive changes in their lives improve their situation and recover. Even if you have received treatment for a disorder before, or if you've already made attempts to solve your problems, you should know that it's often necessary to try several different solutions before the right solution or combination of solutions can be found. Almost all problems can be treated or resolved.

Why suicide can seem like the only option

If you are unable to think of solutions other than suicide, it is not that other solutions don't exist, but rather that you are currently unable to see them. The intense emotional pain that you're experiencing right now can distort your thinking so it becomes harder to see possible solutions to problems, or to connect with those who can offer support. Therapists, counselors, or friends or loved ones, can help you to see solutions that otherwise may not be apparent to you. Give them a chance to help.

A suicidal crisis is almost always temporary

Although it might seem as if your pain and unhappiness will never end, it is important to realize that crises are usually temporary. Solutions are often found, feelings change, unexpected positive events occur. Remember: suicide is a permanent solution to a temporary problem. Give yourself the time necessary for things to change and the pain to subside.

Reaching out for help

Even if it doesn't feel like it right now, **there are many people who want to support you during this difficult time.** They won't try to argue with you about how miserable you feel or tell you to just "snap out of it." They will not judge you. They will simply listen to you and be there for you.

Reach out to someone. Do it now. If you promised yourself 24-hours or a week in step #1, use that time to tell someone what's going on with you. You can call a trusted friend, family member, minister, rabbi, doctor, or therapist. It doesn't matter who it is, as long as it's someone you trust and who is likely to listen with compassion and acceptance.

If you don't know who to turn to:

In the U.S. —Call the National Suicide Prevention Lifeline at 1-800-273-TALK (8255) or the National Hopeline Network at 1-800-SUICIDE (1-800-784-2433). These toll-free crisis hotlines offer 24-hour suicide prevention and support. Your call is free and confidential.
Outside the U.S. —Visit IASP or Suicide.org to find a helpline in your country.
How to talk to someone about your suicidal thoughts
Even when you've decided who you

can trust to talk to, admitting your suicidal thoughts to another person can be difficult.

> Tell the person exactly what you are telling yourself. If you have a suicide plan, explain it to them.

> Phrases such as, "I can't take it anymore" or "I'm done" are vague and do not illustrate how serious things really are. Tell the person you trust that you are thinking about suicide.

> If it is too difficult for you to talk about, try writing it down and handing a note to the person you trust. Or send them an email or text and sit with them while they read it.

What if you don't feel understood?

If you do not feel the person you have chosen to talk to has understood, tell someone else, or call a suicide crisis helpline. There are plenty of people out there who will understand. Don't let one bad experience stop you from finding someone who can help.

Ways to cope with suicidal thoughts and feelings

Remember that while it may seem as if these suicidal thoughts and feelings will never end, this is never a permanent condition. **You WILL feel better again.** In the meantime, there are some ways to help cope with your suicidal thoughts and feelings.

Things To Do:

Talk with someone every day, preferably face to face. Though you feel like withdrawing, ask trusted friends and acquaintances to spend time with you. Or continue to call a crisis helpline and talk about your feelings.

Make a safety plan. Develop a set of steps that you can follow during a suicidal crisis. It should include contact numbers for your doctor or therapist, as well as friends and family members who will help in an emergency.

Make a written schedule for yourself every day and stick to it, no matter what. Keep a regular routine as much as possible, even when your feelings seem out of control.

Get out in the sun or into nature for at least 30 minutes a day.

Exercise as vigorously as is safe for you . To get the most benefit, aim for 30 minutes of exercise per day. But you can start small. Three 10-minute bursts of activity can have a positive effect on mood.

Make time for things that bring you joy. Even if very few things bring you pleasure at the moment, force yourself to do the things you used to enjoy.

Remember your personal goals. You may have always wanted to travel to a particular place, read a specific book, own a pet, move to another place, learn a new hobby, volunteer, go back to school, or start a family. Write your personal goals down.

Things to avoid:

Being alone. Solitude can make suicidal thoughts even worse. Visit a friend, or family member, or pick up the phone and call a crisis helpline.

Alcohol and drugs. Drugs and alcohol can increase depression, hamper your problem-solving ability, and can make you act impulsively.

Doing things that make you feel worse. Listening to sad music, looking at certain photographs, reading old letters, or visiting a loved one's grave can all increase negative feelings.

Thinking about suicide and other negative thoughts. Try not to become preoccupied with suicidal thoughts as this can make them even stronger. Don't think and rethink negative thoughts. Find a distraction. Giving yourself a break from suicidal thoughts can help, even if it's for a short time.

Recovering from suicidal feelings

Even if your suicidal thoughts and feelings have subsided, get help for yourself. Experiencing that sort of emotional pain is itself a traumatizing experience. Finding a support group or therapist can be very helpful in decreasing the chances that you will feel suicidal again in the future. You can get help and referrals from your doctor or from the organizations listed in our Related Links section.

5 steps to recovering from suicidal thoughts and feelings

Identify triggers or situations that lead to feelings of despair or generate suicidal thoughts, such as an anniversary of a loss, alcohol, or stress from relationships. Find ways to avoid these places, people, or situations.

Take care of yourself. Eat right, don't skip meals, and get plenty of sleep. Exercise is also key:

it releases endorphins, relieves stress, and promotes emotional well-being.

Build your support network. Surround yourself with positive influences and people who make you feel good about yourself. The more you're invested in other people and your community, the more you have to lose-which will help you stay positive and on the recovery track.

Develop new activities and interests. Find new hobbies, volunteer activities, or work that gives you a sense of meaning and purpose. When you're doing things you find fulfilling, you'll feel better about yourself and feelings of despair are less likely to return.

Learn to deal with stress in a healthy way. Find healthy ways to keep your stress levels in check, including exercising, meditating, using sensory strategies to relax, practicing simple breathing exercises, and challenging self-defeating thoughts.

More help for dealing with suicidal thoughts and feelings
Suicide Prevention: How to Help Someone who is Suicidal
Depression Symptoms and Warning Signs: How to Recognize Depression Symptoms and Get Effective Help
Bipolar Disorder Signs and Symptoms: Recognizing Mania, Hypomania and Bipolar Depression
Guide for Teen Depression: Learn

Tips and Tools for Helping Yourself or a Friend
 Depression in Older Adults: Recognize the Signs and Find Treatment that Works
 Dealing with Depression: Self-Help and Coping Tips to Overcome Depression

Resources and References
Suicide crisis lines and help for suicidal thoughts
National Suicide Prevention Lifeline —Suicide prevention telephone hotline funded by the U.S. government. Provides free, 24-hour assistance. 1-800-273-TALK (8255). (National Suicide Prevention Lifeline)
National Hopeline Network —Toll-free telephone number offering 24-hour suicide crisis support. 1-800-SUICIDE (784-2433).

(National Hopeline Network)

The Trevor Project —Crisis intervention and suicide prevention services for lesbian, gay, bisexual, transgender, and questioning (LGBTQ) youth. Includes a 24/7 hotline: 1-866-488-7386.

State Prevention Programs — Browse through a database of suicide prevention programs, organized by state. (National Strategy for Suicide Prevention)

Crisis Centers in Canada —Locate suicide crisis centers in Canada by province. (Canadian Association for Suicide Prevention)

Befrienders Worldwide — International suicide prevention organization connects people to crisis hotlines in their country.

IASP —Find crisis centers and helplines around the world. (International Association for Suicide

Prevention).

<u>International Suicide Hotlines</u> —
Find a helpline in different countries
around the world. (Suicide.org)

<u>Samaritans UK</u> —24-hour suicide
support for people in the UK (call
08457 90 90 90) and Ireland (call
1850 60 90 90). (Samaritans)

<u>Lifeline Australia</u> —24-hour suicide
crisis support service at 13 11 14.
(Lifeline Australia)

If you are feeling suicidal

<u>If you are thinking about suicide,
read this first</u> —Tips for getting
you through when you're feeling
suicidal, as well as information about
maintaining recovery and healing.
(Metanoia)

<u>About Suicide</u> —UK National Health
Service site offering information
for those considering suicide or
have attempted suicide in the past.

(Moodjuice)

Coping with suicidal thoughts —
PDF download with information
on how to understand your suicidal
feelings and how to develop a safety
plan. (Consortium for Organizational
Mental Health)
Authors: Jaelline Jaffe, Ph.D.,
Lawrence Robinson, and Jeanne Segal,
Ph.D. Last updated: April 2015.
©Helpguide.org. All rights
reserved. This reprint is for
information only and NOT
a substitute for professional
diagnosis and treatment.
Helpguide.org is an ad-free nonprofit resource for supporting
better mental health and lifestyle
choices for adults and children.

USED WITH PERMISSION

APPENDIX D

Suicide Prevention
How to Help Someone who is Suicidal

A suicidal person may not ask for help, but that doesn't mean that help isn't wanted. Most people who commit suicide don't want to die-they just want to stop hurting. Suicide prevention starts with recognizing the warning signs and taking them seriously. If you think a friend or family member is considering suicide, you might be afraid to bring up the subject. But talking openly about suicidal thoughts and feelings can save a life.

If you're thinking about committing suicide, please read Suicide Help or call 1-800-273-TALK in the U.S.!

To find a suicide helpline outside the U.S., visit <u>IASP</u> or <u>Suicide.org</u> .

Understanding and preventing suicide

The World Health Organization estimates that approximately 1 million people die each year from suicide. What drives so many individuals to take their own lives? To those not in the grips of suicidal <u>depression</u> and despair, it's difficult to understand what drives so many individuals to take their own lives. But a suicidal person is in so much pain that he or she can see no other option.

Suicide is a desperate attempt to escape suffering that has become unbearable. Blinded by feelings of self-loathing, hopelessness, and isolation, a suicidal person can't see any way of finding relief except through death. But despite their desire for the pain to stop, most suicidal people are deeply conflicted about ending their own lives. They wish there was an alternative to committing suicide, but they just can't see one.

Common Misconceptions about Suicide

FALSE: People who talk about suicide won't really do it.

Almost everyone who commits or attempts suicide has given some clue or warning. Do not ignore suicide threats. Statements like "you'll be sorry when I'm dead," "I can't see any way out,"—no matter how casually or jokingly said may indicate serious suicidal feelings.

FALSE: Anyone who tries to kill him/herself must be crazy.

Most suicidal people are not psychotic or insane. They must be upset, grief-stricken, depressed or despairing, but extreme distress and emotional pain are not necessarily signs of mental illness.

FALSE: If a person is determined to kill him/herself, nothing is going to stop them.

Even the most severely depressed person has mixed feelings about death, wavering until the very last moment between wanting to live and wanting to die. Most suicidal people do not want death; they want the pain to stop. The impulse to end it all, however overpowering, does not last forever.

FALSE: People who commit suicide are people who were unwilling to seek help.

Studies of suicide victims have shown that more than half had sought medical help in the six months prior to their deaths.

FALSE: Talking about suicide may give someone the idea.

You don't give a suicidal person morbid ideas by talking about suicide. The opposite is true—bringing up the subject of suicide and discussing it openly is one of the most helpful things you can do.

Source: *SAVE - Suicide Awareness Voices of Education*

Warning Signs of Suicide

Most suicidal individuals give warning signs or signals of their intentions. The best way to prevent suicide is to recognize these warning signs and know how to respond if you spot them. If you believe that a friend or family member is suicidal, you can play a role in suicide prevention by pointing out the alternatives, showing that you care, and getting a doctor or psychologist involved.

Major warning signs for suicide include talking about killing or harming oneself, talking or writing a lot about death or dying, and seeking out things that could be used in a suicide attempt, such as weapons and drugs. These signals are even more dangerous if the person has a mood disorder such as depression or bipolar disorder, suffers from alcohol dependence, has previously attempted suicide, or has a family history of suicide.

Take any suicidal talk or behavior seriously. It's not just a warning sign that the person is thinking about suicide-**it's a cry for help.**

A more subtle but equally dangerous warning sign of suicide is hopelessness. Studies have found that hopelessness is a strong predictor of suicide. People who feel hopeless may talk about "unbearable" feelings, predict a bleak future, and state that they have nothing to look forward to.

Other warning signs that point to a suicidal mind frame include dramatic mood swings or sudden personality changes, such as going from outgoing to withdrawn or well-behaved to rebellious. A suicidal person may also lose interest in day-to-day activities, neglect his or her appearance, and show big changes in eating or sleeping habits.

Suicide Warning Signs

- Talking about suicide, any talk about suicide, dying, or self-harm, such as "I wish I hadn't been born," "If I see you again..." and "I'd be better off dead."

- Seeking out lethal means

- Seeking access to guns, pills, knives, or other objects that could be used in a suicide attempt.

- Preoccupation with death

- Unusual focus on death, dying, or violence. Writing poems or stories about death.

- No hope for the future

- Feelings of helplessness, hopelessness, and being trapped ("There's no way out"). Belief that things will never get better or change.

- Self-loathing, self-hatred

- Feelings of worthlessness, guilt, shame, and self-hatred. Feeling like a burden ("Everyone would be better off without me").

- Getting affairs in order

- Making out a will. Giving away prized possessions. Making arrangements for family members.

- Saying goodbye

- Unusual or unexpected visits or calls to family and friends. Saying goodbye to people as if they won't be seen again.

- Withdrawing from others

- Withdrawing from friends and family. Increasing social isolation. Desire to be left alone.

- Self-destructive behavior

- Increased alcohol or drug use, reckless driving, unsafe sex. Taking unnecessary risks as if they have a "death wish."

- Sudden sense of calm, a sudden sense of calm and happiness after being extremely depressed can mean that the person has made a decision to commit suicide.

Suicide Warning Signs

Talking about suicide-
Any talk about suicide, dying, or self-harm, such as "I wish I hadn't been born," "If I see you again..." and "I'd be better off dead."

Seeking out lethal means-
Seeking access to guns, pills, knives, or other objects that could be used in a suicide attempt.

Preoccupation with death-
Unusual focus on death, dying, or violence. Writing poems or stories about death.

No hope for the future-
Feelings of helplessness, hopelessness, and being trapped ("There's no way out"). Belief that things will never get better or change.

Self-loathing, self-hatred-
Feelings of worthlessness, guilt, shame, and self-hatred. Feeling like a burden ("Everyone would be better off

without me").

Getting affairs in order-
Making out a will. Giving away prized possessions. Making arrangements for family members.

Saying goodbye-
Unusual or unexpected visits or calls to family and friends. Saying goodbye to people as if they won't be seen again.

Withdrawing from others-
Withdrawing from friends and family. Increasing social isolation. Desire to be left alone.

Self-destructive behavior-
Increased alcohol or drug use, reckless driving, unsafe sex. Taking unnecessary risks as if they have a "death wish." Sudden sense of calm A sudden sense of calm and happiness after being extremely depressed can mean that the person has made a decision to commit suicide.

Suicide prevention tip #1: Speak up if you're worried

If you spot the warning signs of suicide in someone you care about, you may wonder if it's a good idea to say anything. What if you're wrong? What if the person gets angry? In such situations, it's natural to feel uncomfortable or afraid. But anyone who talks about suicide or shows other warning signs needs immediate help- the sooner the better.

Talking to a person about suicide

Talking to a friend or family member about their suicidal thoughts and feelings can be extremely difficult for anyone. But if you're unsure whether someone is suicidal, the best way to find out is to ask. You can't make a person suicidal by showing that you care. In fact, giving a suicidal person the opportunity to express his or her feelings can provide relief from loneliness and pent-up negative feelings, and may prevent a suicide attempt.

Ways to start a conversation about suicide:
- I have been feeling concerned about you lately.
- Recently, I have noticed some differences in you and wondered how you are doing.
- I wanted to check in with you because you haven't seemed yourself lately.

Questions you can ask:
- When did you begin feeling like this?
- Did something happen that made you start feeling this way?
- How can I best support you right now?

- Have you thought about getting help?

What you can say that helps:
- You are not alone in this. I'm here for you.
- You may not believe it now, but the way you're feeling will change.
- I may not be able to understand exactly how you feel, but I care about you and want to help.
- When you want to give up, tell yourself you will hold off for just one more day, hour, minute- whatever you can manage.

When talking to a suicidal person Do:
- Be yourself. Let the person know you care, that he/she is not alone. The right words are often unimportant. If you

are concerned, your voice and manner will show it.

- Listen. Let the suicidal person unload despair, ventilate anger. No matter how negative the conversation seems, the fact that it exists is a positive sign.
- Be sympathetic, non-judgmental, patient, calm, accepting. Your friend or family member is doing the right thing by talking about his/her feelings.
- Offer hope. Reassure the person that help is available and that the suicidal feelings are temporary. Let the person know that his or her life is important to you.
- If the person says things like, "I'm so depressed, I can't go on," ask the question: "Are you having thoughts of suicide?" You are not putting ideas in their head, you are showing that you

are concerned, that you take them seriously, and that it's OK for them to share their pain with you.

But don't:

- Argue with the suicidal person. Avoid saying things like: "You have so much to live for," "Your suicide will hurt your family," or "Look on the bright side."
- Act shocked, lecture on the value of life, or say that suicide is wrong.
- Promise confidentiality. Refuse to be sworn to secrecy. A life is at stake and you may need to speak to a mental health professional in order to keep the suicidal person safe. If you promise to keep your discussions secret, you may have to break your word.
- Offer ways to fix their problems,

or give advice, or make them feel like they have to justify their suicidal feelings. It is not about how bad the problem is, but how badly it's hurting your friend or loved one.

- Blame yourself. You can't "fix" someone's depression. Your loved one's happiness, or lack thereof, is not your responsibility.

Adapted from: *Metanoia.org*

Suicide prevention tip #2: Respond quickly in a crisis
If a friend or family member tells you that he or she is thinking about death or suicide, it's important to evaluate the immediate danger the person is in. Those at the highest risk for committing suicide in the near future have a specific suicide PLAN, the MEANS to carry out the plan,

a TIME SET for doing it, and an INTENTION to do it.

Level of Suicide Risk

Low—Some suicidal thoughts. No suicide plan. Says he or she won't commit suicide.

Moderate—Suicidal thoughts. Vague plan that isn't very lethal. Says he or she won't commit suicide.

High—Suicidal thoughts. Specific plan that is highly lethal. Says he or she won't commit suicide.

Severe—Suicidal thoughts. Specific plan that is highly lethal. Says he or she will commit suicide.

The following questions can help you assess the immediate risk for suicide:

- Do you have a suicide plan? (PLAN)
- Do you have what you need to carry out your plan (pills, gun,

etc.)? (MEANS)
- Do you know when you would do it? (TIME SET)
- Do you intend to commit suicide? (INTENTION)

If a suicide attempt seems imminent, call a local crisis center, dial 911, or take the person to an emergency room. Remove guns, drugs, knives, and other potentially lethal objects from the vicinity but **do not, under any circumstances, leave a suicidal person alone.**

Suicide prevention tip #3: Offer help and support

If a friend or family member is suicidal, the best way to help is by offering an empathetic, listening ear. Let your loved one know that he or she is not alone and that you care. Don't take responsibility, however, for making your loved one well. You can offer support, but you can't get better for a suicidal person. He or she has to make a personal commitment to recovery.

It takes a lot of courage to help someone who is suicidal. Witnessing a loved one dealing with thoughts about ending his or her own life can stir up many difficult emotions. As you're helping a suicidal person, don't forget to take care of yourself. Find someone that you trust-a friend, family member, clergyman, or counselor-to talk to about your feelings and get support of your own.

Helping a suicidal person:
  Get professional help. Do
    everything in your power to get
    a suicidal person the help he or
    she needs. Call a crisis line for

advice and referrals. Encourage the person to see a mental health professional, help locate a treatment facility, or take them to a doctor's appointment.

Follow-up on treatment. If the doctor prescribes medication, make sure your friend or loved one takes it as directed. Be aware of possible side effects and be sure to notify the physician if the person seems to be getting worse. It often takes time and persistence to find the medication or therapy that's right for a particular person.

Be proactive. Those contemplating suicide often don't believe they can be helped, so you may have to be more proactive at offering assistance. Saying, "Call me if you need anything" is too vague. Don't wait for the person to call you or even to return your calls. Drop by, call again, invite the person out.

Encourage positive lifestyle changes, such as a healthy diet, plenty of sleep, and getting out in the sun or into nature for at least 30 minutes each day. Exercise is also extremely important as it releases endorphins, relieves stress, and promotes emotional well-being.

Make a safety plan. Help the person develop a set of steps he or she promises to follow during a suicidal crisis. It should identify any triggers that may lead to a suicidal crisis, such as an anniversary of a loss, alcohol, or stress from relationships. Also include contact numbers for the person's doctor or therapist, as well as friends and family members who will help in an emergency.

Remove potential means of suicide, such as pills, knives, razors, or firearms. If the person is likely to take an overdose, keep medications locked away or give out only as the person needs them.

Continue your support over the long haul. Even after the immediate suicidal crisis has passed, stay in touch with the person, periodically checking in or dropping by. Your support is vital to ensure your friend or loved one remains on the recovery track.

Risk factors for suicide

According to the U.S. Department of Health and Human Services, at least

90 percent of all people who commit suicide suffer from one or more mental disorders such as depression, bipolar disorder, schizophrenia, or alcoholism. Depression in particular plays a large role in suicide. The difficulty suicidal people have imagining a solution to their suffering is due in part to the distorted thinking caused by depression.

Antidepressants and Suicide

For some, depression medication causes an increase-rather than a decrease-in depression and suicidal thoughts and feelings. Because of this risk, the FDA advises that anyone on antidepressants should be watched for increases in suicidal thoughts and behaviors. Monitoring is especially important if this is the person's first time on depression medication or if the dose has recently been changed. **The risk of suicide is the greatest during the first two months of antidepressant treatment.**

Common suicide risk factors include:
- Mental illness
- Alcoholism or drug abuse
- Previous suicide attempts
- Family history of suicide
- Terminal illness or chronic pain

- Recent loss or stressful life event
- Social isolation and loneliness
- History of trauma or abuse

Suicide in teens and older adults

In addition to the general risk factors for suicide, both teenagers and older adults are at a higher risk of suicide.

Suicide in Teens

Teenage suicide is a serious and growing problem. The teenage years can be emotionally turbulent and stressful. Teenagers face pressures to succeed and fit in. They may struggle with self-esteem issues, self-doubt, and feelings of alienation. For some, this leads to suicide. Depression is also a major risk factor for teen suicide.

Other risk factors for teenage suicide include:

- Childhood abuse
- Recent traumatic event
- Lack of a support network
- Availability of a gun
- Hostile social or school environment
- Exposure to other teen suicides

Suicide warning signs in teens
Additional warning signs that a teen may be considering suicide:
- Change in eating and sleeping habits
- Withdrawal from friends, family, and regular activities
- Violent or rebellious behavior, running away
- Drug and alcohol use
- Unusual neglect of personal appearance
- Persistent boredom, difficulty concentrating, or a decline in the quality of schoolwork

- Frequent complaints about physical symptoms, often related to emotions, such as stomachaches, headaches, fatigue, etc.
- Not tolerating praise or rewards

Source: *American Academy of Child & Adolescent Psychiatry*

Suicide in the Elderly

The highest suicide rates of any age group occur among persons aged 65 years and older. One contributing factor is depression in the elderly that is undiagnosed and untreated.

Other risk factors for suicide in the elderly include:
- Recent death of a loved one
- Physical illness, disability, or pain

- Isolation and loneliness Major life changes, such as retirement
- Loss of independence
- Loss of sense of purpose **Suicide warning signs in older adults**

Additional warning signs that an elderly person may be contemplating suicide:

- Reading material about death and suicide
- Disruption of sleep patterns
- Increased alcohol or prescription drug use
- Failure to take care of self or follow medical orders
- Stockpiling medications
- Sudden interest in firearms
- Social withdrawal or elaborate good-byes
- Rush to complete or revise a will

Source: *University of Florida*

More help for suicide prevention
Suicide Help: How to Help Someone who is Suicidal
Depression Symptoms and Warning Signs: How to Recognize Depression Symptoms and Get Effective Help
Helping a Depressed Person: How to Reach Out and Help Someone While Taking Care of Yourself
Guide for Teen Depression: Learn Tips and Tools for Helping Yourself or a Friend
Helping Loved Ones with Bipolar Disorder: Bipolar Disorder in Children, Teens, and Family Members
Help for Parents of Troubled Teens: Dealing with Anger, Violence, Delinquency, and Other Teen Behavior Problems
Resources and References
General information about suicide
Understanding Suicidal Thinking

(PDF)—Learn about preventing
suicide attempts and offering help
and support. (Depression and Bipolar
Support Alliance)

Suicide in America: Frequently
Asked Questions —Find answers to
common questions about suicide,
including who is at the highest risk
and how to help. (National Institute
of Mental Health)

Suicide and Mental Illness —Facts
on the link between suicide and
mental illnesses such as depression,
substance abuse, schizophrenia, and
bipolar disorder. (StopaSuicide.org)

Suicide   and Suicide in Youth —
Suicide fact sheets answer questions
about whose at risk and what friends
and family can do to prevent suicide.
(The National Alliance for the
Mentally Ill).

Helping a suicidal person

<u>What Can I Do To Help Someone Who Might be Suicidal?</u>—Discusses possible warning signs of suicidal thoughts and ways to prevent suicide attempts. (Metanoia)

<u>Frequently Asked Questions</u> — Questions and answers about suicide prevention, including what you should do if you're worried and what to do if someone refuses help. (American Foundation for Suicide Prevention)

<u>Handling a Call From a Suicidal Person</u> —How to handle a phone call from a friend or family member who is suicidal. Features tips on what to say and how to help. (Metanoia.org)

Suicide hotlines and crisis support

<u>National Suicide Prevention Lifeline</u> —Suicide prevention telephone hotline funded by the U.S.

government. Provides free, 24-hour assistance. 1-800-273-TALK (8255).
National Hope line Network — Toll-free telephone number offering 24-hour suicide crisis support. 1-800-SUICIDE (784-2433). (National Hopeline Network)
The Trevor Project —Crisis intervention and suicide prevention services for lesbian, gay, bisexual, transgender, and questioning (LGBTQ) youth. Includes a 24/7 hotline: 1-866-488-7386.
State Prevention Programs — Browse through a database of suicide prevention programs, organized by state. (National Strategy for Suicide Prevention)
Crisis Centers in Canada —Locate suicide crisis centers in Canada by province. (Canadian Association for Suicide Prevention)
IASP—Find crisis centers and

helplines around the world. (International Association for Suicide Prevention).
International Suicide Hotlines—Find a helpline in different countries around the world. (Suicide.org)
Befrienders Worldwide—International suicide prevention organization connects people to crisis hotlines in their country. (Befrienders Worldwide)
Samaritans UK—24-hour suicide support for people in the UK (call 08457 90 90 90) and Ireland (call 1850 60 90 90). (Samaritans)
Lifeline Australia —24-hour suicide crisis support service at 13 11 14. (Lifeline Australia)

Coping after a suicide attempt
After an Attempt (PDF)—Guide for taking care of a family member following a suicide attempt and

treatment in an emergency room. (National Suicide Prevention Lifeline)

Authors: Melinda Smith, M.A., Jeanne Segal, Ph.D., and Lawrence Robinson. Last updated: April 2015. ©Helpguide.org. All rights reserved. This site is for information only and NOT a substitute for professional diagnosis and treatment.

USED WITH PERMISSION

APPENDIX E

Grief and Loss

Grief is a natural, yet painful response to loss. There is no right or wrong way to grieve, but there are healthy ways to cope with the pain and express your emotions in ways that allow you to heal.

You may associate grief with the death of a loved one, but any loss can cause grief, including the loss of a relationship, your health, your job, or a cherished dream. After a significant loss, you may experience all kinds of difficult and surprising emotions, such as shock, anger, and guilt.

Everyone grieves differently, but there are healthy ways to cope and heal from the pain.

What is grief?

Are there stages of grief?

Common symptoms of grief

Get support

Take care of yourself

When grief doesn't go away

Professional help

More help

Resources and references

Coping with Grief and Loss

Understanding the Grieving Process

Losing someone or something you love or care deeply about is very painful. You may experience all kinds of difficult emotions and it may feel like the pain and sadness you're experiencing will never let up. These are normal reactions to a significant loss. But while there is no right or wrong way to grieve, there are healthy ways to cope with the pain that, in time, can renew you and permit you to move on.

What is grief?

Grief is a natural response to loss. It's the emotional suffering you feel when something or someone you love is taken away. The more significant the loss, the more intense the grief will be. You may associate grief with the death of a loved one-which is often the cause of the most intense type of grief-but any loss can cause grief, including:

Divorce or relationship breakup

Loss of health

Losing a job

Loss of financial stability

A miscarriage

Retirement Death of a pet

Loss of a cherished dream

A loved one's serious illness

Loss of a friendship

Loss of safety after a trauma

Selling the family home

The more significant the loss, the more intense the grief. However, even subtle losses can lead to grief. For example, you might experience grief after moving away from home, graduating from college, changing jobs, selling your family home, or retiring from a career you loved.

Everyone grieves differently

Grieving is a personal and highly individual experience. How you grieve depends on many factors, including your personality and coping style, your life experience, your faith, and the nature of the loss. The grieving process takes time. Healing happens gradually; it can't be forced or hurried-and **there is no "normal" timetable for grieving.** Some people start to feel better in weeks or months. For others, the grieving process is measured in years. Whatever your grief experience, it's important to be patient with yourself and allow the process to naturally unfold.

Myths and Facts About Grief

MYTH: The pain will go away faster if you ignore it.

Fact: Trying to ignore your pain or keep it from surfacing will only make it worse in the long run. For real healing it is necessary to face your grief and actively deal with it.

MYTH: It's important to be "be strong" in the face of loss.

Fact: Feeling sad, frightened, or lonely is a normal reaction to loss. Crying doesn't mean you are weak. You don't need to "protect" your family or friends by putting on a brave front. Showing your true feelings can help them and you.

MYTH: If you don't cry, it means

you aren't sorry about the loss.

Fact: Crying is a normal response to sadness, but it's not the only one. Those who don't cry may feel the pain just as deeply as others. They may simply have other ways of showing it.

MYTH: Grief should last about a year.

Fact: There is no right or wrong time frame for grieving. How long it takes can differ from person to person.

Source: *Center for Grief and Healing*

Are there stages of grief?

In 1969, psychiatrist Elisabeth Kbler-Ross introduced what became known as the "five stages of grief." These stages of grief were based on her studies of the feelings of patients facing terminal illness, but many people have generalized them to other types of negative life changes and losses, such as the death of a loved one or a break-up.

The five stages of grief:

> **Denial:** "This can't be happening to me."

> **Anger:** "*Why* is this happening? Who is to blame?"

> **Bargaining:** "Make this not happen, and in return I will ____."

> **Depression:** "I'm too sad to do anything."

> **Acceptance:** "I'm at peace with what happened."

If you are experiencing any of these emotions following a loss, it may help to know that your reaction is natural and that you'll heal in time. However, not everyone who grieves goes through all of these stages-and that's okay. Contrary to popular belief, **you**

do not have to go through each stage in order to heal. In fact, some people resolve their grief without going through *any* of these stages. And if you do go through these stages of grief, you probably won't experience them in a neat, sequential order, so don't worry about what you "should" be feeling or which stage you're supposed to be in.

Kbler-Ross herself never intended for these stages to be a rigid framework that applies to everyone who mourns. In her last book before her death in 2004, she said of the five stages of grief: "They were never meant to help tuck messy emotions into neat packages. They are responses to loss that many people have, but **there is not a typical response to loss, as there is no typical loss.** Our grieving is as individual as our lives."

Grief can be a roller coaster

Instead of a series of stages, we

might also think of the grieving process as a roller coaster, full of ups and downs, highs and lows. Like many roller coasters, the ride tends to be rougher in the beginning; the lows may be deeper and longer. The difficult periods should become less intense and shorter as time goes by, but it takes time to work through a loss. Even years after a loss, especially at special events such as a family wedding or the birth of a child, we may still experience a strong sense of grief.

Source: *Hospice Foundation of America*

Common symptoms of grief

While loss affects people in different ways, many experience the following symptoms when they're grieving. Just remember that almost anything that you experience in the early stages of grief is normal-including feeling like you're going crazy, feeling like you're in a bad dream, or questioning your religious beliefs.

Shock and disbelief - Right after a loss, it can be hard to accept what happened. You may feel numb, have trouble believing that the loss really happened, or even deny the truth. If someone you love has died, you may keep expecting him or her to show up, even though you know he or she is gone.

Sadness - Profound sadness is probably the most universally experienced symptom of grief. You may have feelings of emptiness, despair, yearning, or deep loneliness. You may also cry a lot or feel emotionally unstable.

Guilt - You may regret or feel guilty about things you did or didn't say or do. You may also feel guilty about certain feelings (e.g. feeling relieved when the person died after a long, difficult illness). After a death, you may even feel guilty for not doing something to prevent the death, even if there was nothing more you could have done.

Anger - Even if the loss was nobody's fault, you may feel angry and resentful. If you lost a loved one, you may be angry with yourself, God, the doctors, or even the person who died for abandoning you. You may feel the need to blame someone for the injustice that was done to you.

Fear - A significant loss can trigger a host of worries and fears. You may feel anxious, helpless, or insecure. You may even have panic attacks. The death of a loved one can trigger fears about your own mortality, of facing life without that person, or the responsibilities you now face alone.

Physical symptoms - We often think of grief as a strictly emotional process, but grief often involves physical problems, including fatigue, nausea, lowered immunity, weight loss or weight gain, aches and pains, and insomnia.

Coping with grief and loss tip 1: Get support

The single most important factor in healing from loss is having the support of other people. Even if you aren't comfortable talking about your feelings under normal circumstances, it's important to express them when you're grieving. Sharing your loss makes the burden of grief easier to carry. Wherever the support comes from, accept it and **do not grieve alone.** Connecting to others will help you heal.

Finding support after a loss

Turn to friends and family members - Now is the time to lean on the people who care about you, even if you take pride in being strong and self-sufficient. Draw loved ones close, rather than avoiding them, and accept the assistance that's offered. Oftentimes, people want to help but don't know how, so tell them what you need-whether it's a shoulder to cry on or help with funeral arrangements.

Draw comfort from your faith - If you follow a religious tradition, embrace the comfort its mourning rituals can provide. Spiritual activities that are meaningful to you-such as praying, meditating, or going to church-can offer solace. If you're questioning your faith in the wake of the loss, talk to a clergy member or others in your religious community.

Join a support group - Grief can feel very lonely, even when you have loved ones around. Sharing your sorrow with others who have experienced similar losses can help. To find a bereavement support group in your area, contact local hospitals, hospices, funeral homes, and counseling centers.

Talk to a therapist or grief counselor - If your grief feels like too much to bear, call a mental health professional with experience in grief counseling. An experienced therapist can help you work through intense emotions and overcome obstacles to your grieving.

Coping with grief and loss tip 2:

Take care of yourself

When you're grieving, it's more important than ever to take care of yourself. The stress of a major loss can quickly deplete your energy and emotional reserves. Looking after your physical and emotional needs will help you get through this difficult time.

Face your feelings. You can try to suppress your grief, but you can't avoid it forever. In order to heal, you have to acknowledge the pain. Trying to avoid feelings of sadness and loss only prolongs the grieving process. Unresolved grief can also lead to complications such as depression, anxiety, substance abuse, and health problems.

Express your feelings in a tangible or creative way. Write about your loss in a journal. If you've lost a loved one, write a letter saying the things you never got to say; make a scrapbook or photo album celebrating the person's life; or get involved in a cause or organization that was important to him or her.

Look after your physical health. The mind and body are connected. When you feel good physically, you'll also feel better emotionally. Combat stress and fatigue by getting enough sleep, eating right, and exercising. Don't use alcohol or drugs to numb the pain of grief or lift your mood artificially.

Don't let anyone tell you how to feel, and don't tell yourself how to feel either. Your grief is your own, and no one else can tell you when it's time to "move on" or "get over it." Let yourself feel whatever you feel without embarrassment or judgment. It's okay to be angry, to yell at the heavens, to cry or not to cry. It's also okay to laugh, to find moments of joy, and to let go when you're ready.

Plan ahead for grief "triggers." Anniversaries, holidays, and milestones can reawaken memories and feelings. Be prepared for an emotional wallop, and know that it's completely normal. If you're sharing a holiday or lifecycle event with other relatives, talk to them ahead of time about their expectations and agree on strategies to honor the person you loved.

Using social media for support

Memorial pages on Facebook and other social media sites have become popular ways to inform a wide audience of a loved one's passing and to reach out for support. As well as allowing you to impart practical information, such as funeral plans, these pages allow friends and loved ones to post their own tributes or condolences. Reading such messages can often provide some comfort for those grieving the loss.

Of course, posting sensitive content on social media has its risks as well. Memorial pages are often open to anyone with a Facebook account. This may encourage people who hardly knew the deceased to post well-meaning but inappropriate comments or advice. Worse, memorial pages can also attract internet trolls. There have been many well-publicized cases of strangers posting cruel or abusive messages on Facebook memorial pages.

To gain some protection, you can opt to create a closed group on Facebook rather than a public page, which means people have to be approved by a group member before they can access the memorial. It's also important to remember that while social media can be a useful tool for reaching out to others, it can't replace the face-to-face connection and support you need at this time.

When grief doesn't go away

It's normal to feel sad, numb, or angry following a loss. But as time passes, these emotions should become less intense as you accept the loss and start to move forward. If you aren't feeling better over time, or your grief is getting worse, it may be a sign that your grief has developed into a more serious problem, such as complicated grief or major depression.

Complicated grief

The sadness of losing someone you love never goes away completely, but it shouldn't remain center stage. If the pain of the loss is so constant and severe that it keeps you from resuming your life, you may be suffering from a condition known as *complicated grief*. Complicated grief is like being stuck in an intense state of mourning. You may have trouble accepting the death long after it has occurred or be so preoccupied with the person who died that it disrupts your daily routine and undermines your other relationships.

Symptoms of complicated grief include:

- Intense longing and yearning for the deceased

- Intrusive thoughts or images of your loved one

- Denial of the death or sense of disbelief

- Imagining that your loved one is alive Searching for the person in familiar places

- Avoiding things that remind

you of your loved one

- Extreme anger or bitterness over the loss

- Feeling that life is empty or meaningless

The difference between grief and depression

Distinguishing between grief and clinical depression isn't always easy as they share many symptoms, but there are ways to tell the difference. Remember, grief can be a roller coaster. It involves a wide variety of emotions and a mix of good and bad days. Even when you're in the middle of the grieving process, you will have moments of pleasure or happiness. With depression, on the other hand, the feelings of emptiness and despair are constant.

Other symptoms that suggest depression, not just grief:

- Intense, pervasive sense of guilt
- Thoughts of suicide or a preoccupation with dying
- Feelings of hopelessness or worthlessness Slow speech and body movements
- Inability to function at work, home, and/or school
- Seeing or hearing things that aren't there

Can antidepressants help grief?

As a general rule, normal grief does not warrant the use of antidepressants. While medication may relieve some of the symptoms of grief, it cannot treat the cause, which is the loss itself. Furthermore, by numbing the pain that must be worked through eventually, antidepressants delay the mourning process.

When to seek professional help for grief

If you recognize any of the above symptoms of complicated grief or clinical depression, talk to a mental health professional right away. Left untreated, complicated grief and depression can lead to significant emotional damage, life-threatening health problems, and even suicide. But treatment can help you get better.

Contact a grief counselor or professional therapist if you:

- Feel like life isn't worth living

- Wish you had died with your loved one

- Blame yourself for the loss or for failing to prevent it

- Feel numb and disconnected from others for more than a few weeks

- Are having difficulty trusting others since your loss

- Are unable to perform your

normal daily activities

More help for coping with grief and loss

Grief and Loss Help Center: There is no right or wrong way to grieve, but there are healthy ways to cope with the pain and express your emotions in ways that allow you to heal.

Coping with grief and loss help

Supporting a Grieving Person: Understanding the Grieving Process

Coping with Pet Loss: Grieving the Death of a Dog or Cat and Moving On

Coping with a Breakup or Divorce: Moving on After a Relationship Ends

Saying Goodbye: Coping With a Loved One's Terminal Illness

Related Issues

Depression Symptoms

and Warning Signs: How
to Recognize Depression
Symptoms and Get Effective
Help

 Emotional and Psychological
Trauma: Symptoms, Treatment,
and Recovery

 Traumatic Stress: How to
Recover From Disasters and
Other Traumatic Events

 Post-Traumatic Stress Disorder
(PTSD): Symptoms, Treatment
and Self-Help for PTSD

Resources and references

General information about grief and loss

Life after Loss: Dealing with Grief -
Guide to coping with grief and loss,
including normal grief reactions
to expect. (University of Texas
Counseling and Mental Health
Center)

<u>Death and Grief</u> - Article for teens on how to cope with grief and loss. Includes tips for dealing with the pain and taking care of yourself during the grieving process. (Nemours Foundation)

Death of a loved one

<u>Grief: Coping With Reminders After a Loss</u> - Tips for coping with the grief that can resurface even years after you've lost a loved one. (Mayo Clinic)

<u>On Being Alone: A Guide for the Newly Widowed</u> - A comprehensive series of articles on grief and loss offering practical, as well as psychological advice. (AARP)

Support for grief and loss

<u>GriefNet.org</u> - Online support community for people dealing with grief, death, and major loss, with over fifty monitored support groups for both kids and adults. (GriefNet.

org)

Compassionate Friends - National, self-help organization for those grieving the loss of a child. Includes a Chapter Locator   and supportive online brochures   on various aspects of grief. (The Compassionate Friends)

Using Facebook to Grieve - Article about using Facebook memorial pages to grieve a loved one. (Coping with Loss and Grief)

Stages of grief

The Kbler-Ross Grief Cycle - Details each stage as it applies to persons facing death or other negative life change. Note that the cycle as presented includes seven stages, including initial shock. (ChangingMinds.org)

What is Grief? - Lays out general stages of grief with tips for helping someone who is grieving. (University of Illinois Counseling Center)

Complicated grief and depression

<u>Major Depression and Complicated Grief</u> - Lists the warning signs and symptoms that suggest grief has progressed to major depression or complicated grief. (American Cancer Society)

<u>Complicated Grief</u> - Learn the difference between the normal grief reaction and complicated grief. Includes information about symptoms, risk factors, and treatment. (Harvard Medical School Family Health Guide)

Grief after suicide

<u>Grief after Suicide</u> - Understanding your emotions, as well as suicide in general, may ease your grieving after suicide. (Buddha Dharma Education Association)

Helping others cope

Supporting a Grieving Person: Helping Others Through Grief, Loss, and Bereavement

Featured articles

Coping with Grief and Loss:
Losing someone or something you love is very painful. At times, you may feel like you're on an emotional roller coaster. Explore healthy ways to work through your feelings and find healing and renewal. MORE

Supporting a Grieving Person:
You may not know what to say or do when someone you care about is grieving, but you don't need to have answers. There are many ways to help, starting with simply being there and letting the person know you care. MORE

Coping with a Breakup or Divorce:
It's never easy when a relationship ends. But even in the midst of the

sadness and stress of a divorce or breakup, you have an opportunity to learn from the experience and grow into a stronger, wiser person. **MORE**

Helpguide.org. All rights reserved. This site is for information only and NOT a substitute for professional diagnosis and treatment.

USED WITH PERMISSION

APPENDIX F

Comforting Others with the Comfort which we ourselves have been comforted by God (see II Corinthians 1: 3-4).

COPING WITH SUICIDE LOSS

American Foundation for Suicide Prevention (AFSP)

Understanding and preventing suicide through research, education, and advocacy.

Coping with Suicide Loss

If someone you love has died by suicide, you are not alone. There are, sadly, many others who share your sorrow and questions.

We are here to:

- Help all who are bereaved find the support they need and deserve.

- Honor our loved ones and remember them by how they lived, not only how they died.

- Provide volunteer opportunities for survivors of suicide loss to get involved in ways that make sense to them.

If you are new to our community and this site, please take the time to explore the resources and programs provided here. You are in a safe place with people who understand. People who have survived the suicide of a loved one are among the most courageous people we know. **Be well, be peaceful, be hopeful.**

Find Support

People who have lost a family member, friend, classmate, or colleague to suicide often benefit from sharing their experiences with others who have lived through similar losses and/or from seeking

the help of a mental health professional.

Below are resources to help you heal by connecting you with those who understand the challenges of finding your way in the aftermath of a suicide:

• In-Person Support Groups for Suicide Loss Survivors
• Online Support Groups for Suicide Loss Survivors
• Advice on How to Find a Therapist
• Peer Visits with a Trained Suicide Loss Survivor: upon request, AFSP's Survivor Outreach Program provides peer support to the recently bereaved
• AFSP's International Survivors of Suicide Loss Day: attend one of hundreds of local healing events in cities around the world
• Join our Survivor eNetwork: add your email address to our mailing

list so we can keep you updated on programs and events of interest to the suicide loss survivor community Other Organizations that Provide Support

• Engaging People With Lived Experience

Engaging People With Lived Experience

03/06/2015

At AFSP, we believe that the millions of people with lived experience of suicidal ideation and behavior can be passionate stakeholders in the fight against suicide.

• Frequently Asked Questions
• Find Help
• Treatment
• The Interactive Screening Program
• Our Education and Prevention Programs
• Mental Health Tools
• Putting Patients First

- Congressional Spouses for Suicide Prevention and Education
- Where Do I Begin?
- Handling Special Occasions
- Helping Children Understand
- 10 Things You Can Do for Yourself in the Aftermath of a Suicide Loss
- Join the Survivor eNetwork
- Find Support
- International Survivors of Suicide Loss Day
- Education & Training

Handling Special Occasions
Anniversaries, birthdays, holidays, and other occasions after a suicide loss can bring up painful memories, but they also can provide an opportunity to celebrate your loved one.

Anticipating the Event Can Be Harder than the Event Itself

Know that worrying about the event in the time leading up to the event is often more difficult than the event itself.

Communication is Important

Friends and family need to know how to be supportive. If you find it comfortable to talk about your loved one, or would rather grieve in a private way, talk openly with them in advance so that everyone knows what to expect.

It's Okay to Take a Break

If the event proves to be too much, take a short walk. Make sure you have a way to leave early if you need to. Sometimes having an exit strategy can make you feel more at ease.

Consider Traveling

If you have friends or family living in a different city, consider visiting them - a change in scenery might be helpful.

Keep Traditions, or Start New Ones

If holding to longstanding traditions proves too painful, consider developing new family traditions. For example, if you used to cook holiday meals, instead make dinner into a potluck.

Volunteering is a Great Way to Heal

Look online for volunteering opportunities in your area. Many people find meaning in helping others, and it's a great way to honor your loved one.

Sometimes Special Occasions are Just Difficult

Even without the loss of a loved one, occasions like holidays can be stressful. Do the best you can, and remember that healing takes time, and the experience is different for everyone.

Take Care of Yourself

Get enough sleep, eat well, don't drink too much, and practice healthy self-care. Se

Helping Children Understand

When explaining the suicide to a child or adolescent, provide truthful information, encourage questions, and offer loving reassurance.

Talking honestly about suicide does not give others the idea to take their own lives. In fact, understanding mental illness and suicide helps surviving family members to be watchful about their own health, and to take preventative steps when something is wrong.

• Reassure children that they are not responsible, and that nothing they said or did caused anyone else to take their life.

• Be prepared to talk about the suicide multiple times during the first days and weeks, and later throughout the child's life.

• Consider a children's bereavement support group for your child if they are having difficulty adjusting. Learn more about these groups through the Dougy National Center for Grieving Children and Families (www.dougy.org).

For more information about how to talk to children and adolescents, see *Talking to Children About Suicide*, written with the help of two

therapists who lost their mothers
to suicide when they were children.
Other books and information can
be found in the resources section
of our website. Another helpful
guide is *Talking About Suicide*, part
of *After a Suicide: A Toolkit for
Schools*.
Talking to Children About Suicide-
Harpel, Rappaport, Requarth
Joanne Harpel, Margo Requarth, and
Nancy Rappaport. (c) AFSP Survivor
Initiatives Department, 2014.
Talking to Children about Suicide-
Margo Requarth
Margo Requarth, Grief Digest
Magazine, Vol. 4, Issue 4. Reprinted
with permission from Grief Digest,
Center Corp., Omaha, NE, (402)
553-1200.
*Understanding Suicide, Supporting
Children* is a 24-minute film
produced by The Dougy Center. It

provides insight on the emotions and experiences that children, teens and families affected by a suicide death often go through, and offers ways to help. The DVD and guide are a resource for training purposes, or for general viewing by parents, therapists, counselors, and others. Find more information on the Dougy Center website.

10 Things You Can Do for Yourself in the Aftermath of a Suicide Loss

1. Know that everyone grieves in his or her own way and at his or her own pace. There is no timeline or set rhythm for healing.
2. Be kind to yourself and be gentle with yourself.
3. Eat nutritiously and get sufficient rest.
4. Exercise: walk, run, swim, cycle,

etc.

5. Head outdoors and spend time in nature.

6. Give yourself permission to seek professional help—individual and/or family therapy or counseling-and, if applicable to you, call on your personal faith to help you as well.

7. Learn more about the experience of suicide loss by reading the stories of those who are further along in their grief journey.

8. Join a support group or online community for suicide loss survivors.

9. Participate in walks and events such as International Survivors of Suicide Loss Day.

10. Get involved with the survivor loss community by volunteering with an organization such as AFSP.

Used With Permission
Join the Survivor eNetwork
The Survivor eNetwork shares information by email about AFSP resources and initiatives. It is meant for survivors of suicide loss, mental health professionals, and interested others.
• Find Support
• Find a Support Group
• How to Find a Therapist and the Questions to Ask
• Survivor Outreach Program
• Other Organizations that Provide Support
• Information for Support Group Facilitators
Copyright © 2015 American Foundation for Suicide Prevention. All Rights Reserved.
Used With Permission

RESOURCES
Websites, Books, Apps, Videos, Publications, Stats., and More

Suicide Facts at a Glance - Centers for Disease Control 1-800-CDC-INFO (232-4636) cdcinfo@cdc.gov www.cdc.gov/violenceprevention (This website is a Public Domain) Information taken from the CDC website. This resource listing does not constitute the CDCs endorsement of this book or it's contents. The CDC website listing is to assist those who would like additional information.

JASON FOUNDATION, Inc.
The following information and more can be accessed at the Jason Foundation Website:
Parent Resource Program

- <u>Home</u>
- <u>Who's At Risk</u>
- <u>Higher Risk Groups</u>
- <u>Risk Factors</u>
- <u>Elevated Risk Factors</u>
- <u>Facts</u>
- <u>Youth Suicide Statistics</u>
- <u>Signs & Concerns</u>
- <u>Common Myths</u>
- <u>What A Parent Can Do</u>
- <u>Parent and Community Seminar</u>
- <u>Do's and Don'ts</u>
- <u>Resource Library</u>
- <u>About JFI</u>
- <u>Jason's Story</u>
- <u>Programs</u>
- <u>National & Regional Network</u>
- <u>Our Partners</u>
- <u>Contact Us</u>

There is a "Silent Epidemic" sweeping through our nation that claims an average of approximately

100+ young lives each week. It knows no social, racial, or economic barriers. This "Silent Epidemic" is youth suicide! According to the Centers for Disease Control and Prevention's 2013 Youth Risk Behavioral Survey, over ONE out of every THIRTEEN young people in our nation attempted suicide in the previous twelve months. The good news is that twelve out of thirteen did not attempt suicide... but ONE is too many, especially if it is your son or daughter, grandson or granddaughter or the young person next door.

It is our hope that this site will help provide you some of the information, tools and resources to help you identify at-risk youth and know how to assist them in getting help before a tragedy occurs. Prevention begins with education.

Important Disclaimer:

Although The Jason Foundation, Inc. and our partners make every effort to ensure our programs are well formatted and professionally address the problem of youth suicide, no one program can guarantee to prevent youth suicide. Our program's goal is to provide you educational materials that will better help equip you to recognize "signs of concern" that may demonstrate that a young person is possibly struggling with issues that left unaddressed or untreated could result in suicidal ideation. Professional help should always be sought whenever there is a possibility of suicidal ideation. Never try to solve this type of problem without obtaining professional help.

(Information taken from JFI website) This resource listing does not constitute the JFI's endorsement of this book or it's contents. The JFI website listing is to assist those who would like additional information.

PTSD: National Center for PTSD
• PTSD
The following information and more can be accessed at the National Center for PTSD website:

- • PTSD Home
- • For the Public
- • Public Section Home
- • PTSD Overview
- • PTSD Basics
- • Return from War
- • Specific to Women
- • Types of Trauma
- • War
- • Terrorism
- • Violence and Abuse
- • Disasters
- • Is it PTSD?

- Treatment and Coping
- Treatment
- Self-Help and Coping
- PTSD Research
- Where to Get Help for PTSD
- Help with VA PTSD Care or Benefits
- Other Common Problems
- Family and Friends
- PTSD and Communities
- Paginas en Espanol
- Apps, Videos and More
- Mobile Apps
- Videos
- Web Links
- PTSD Site Search
- For Professionals
- Professional Section Home
- PTSD Overview
- Types of Trauma
- Trauma Basics
- Disaster and Terrorism

- <u>Military Trauma</u>
- <u>Violence & other Trauma</u>
- <u>Assessment</u>
- <u>Assessment Overview</u>
- <u>Adult Interviews</u>
- <u>Adult Self Report</u>
- <u>Child Measures</u>
- <u>Deployment Measures</u>
- <u>DSM-5 Validated Measures</u>
- <u>PTSD Screens</u>
- <u>Trauma Exposure Measures</u>
- <u>Assessment Request Form</u>
- <u>List of All Measures</u>
- <u>Treatment</u>
- <u>Treatment Overview</u>
- <u>Early Intervention</u>
- <u>Veterans</u>
- <u>Cultural Considerations</u>
- <u>Women</u>
- <u>Children</u>
- <u>Older Adults</u>
- <u>Working with Families</u>
- <u>PTSD Consultation</u>

• <u>For Specific Providers</u>
• <u>VA Providers and Staff</u>
• <u>Disaster Responders</u>
• <u>Medical Doctors</u>
• <u>Community Providers and Clergy</u>
• <u>Co-Occurring Conditions</u>
• <u>Continuing Education</u>
• <u>Publications</u>
• <u>List of Center Publications</u>
• <u>Articles by Center Staff</u>
• <u>Clinician's Trauma Update</u>
• <u>PTSD Research Quarterly</u>
• <u>Publications Search</u>
• <u>Using the PILOTS Database</u>
• <u>What is PILOTS?</u>
• <u>Quick Search Tips</u>
• <u>Modify Your Search</u>
• <u>How to Obtain Articles</u>
• <u>Alerts</u>
• <u>User Guide</u>
• <u>Purpose and Scope</u>
• <u>Find Assessment Measures</u>

- Instrument Authority List
- Research and Biology
- Research on PTSD
- Biology of PTSD
- Find Materials by Type
- List of Materials By Type
- Assessments
- Continuing Education
- Handouts
- Manuals
- Mobile Apps
- Publications
- Toolkits
- Videos
- Web Links
- Advanced Search
- About Us
- National Center for PTSD

Below are the National Center for PTSD's policies on linking to and from our website.

We welcome any site linking to us as long as the descriptive

**words of our site are accurate
and not misleading and do
not misrepresent an unofficial
relationship between the linking
site and the National Center for
PTSD.**
Information taken from the National
Center for PTSD website. This
resource listing does not constitute
the National Center for PTSDs
endorsement of this book or it's
contents. The National Center for
PTSD website listing is to assist
those who would like additional
information.

AMERICAN FOUNDATION FOR SUICIDE PREVENTION

The following information and more
can be accessed at the American
Foundation for Suicide Prevention
website:
Understanding and preventing

suicide through research, education, and advocacy

- Facts and Figures
- Suicide Warning Signs
- Suicide Risk Factors
- Key Research Findings
- Engaging People With Lived Experience
- Frequently Asked Questions
- Resources

Resources

Statistics

CDC Suicide Prevention Website

The suicide prevention webpage of the Centers for Disease Control and Prevention (CDC) includes a variety of data, reports, awareness materials, and other resources related to suicide and suicide prevention. The CDC also has a public inquiry line at (404) 639-3534.

CDC Wisqars

The latest figures from the Centers

for Disease Control and Prevention (CDC) on completed suicides and self-inflicted injuries come from their Web-based Injury Statistics Query and Reporting System (WISQARS). WISQARS is an interactive, online database that provides statistics related to fatal and nonfatal injury, and is the most authoritative source of suicide-related data. Because it takes time to collect and ensure the accuracy of the data, the data found there may be from two to three years earlier.

World Health Organization
The WHO offers statistical information on suicide in the United States and other countries.
Clinical Information
Medline Plus
The U.S. National Institutes of Health maintains MedlinePlus as a source of medical information for the public.

MedlinePlus's suicide health topics page includes overviews, current suicide information, research, and reference links. The page includes information about treatments and medications, definition of common terms, and medical videos and illustrations. You will also find links there to the latest research, and to information about clinical trials.

Standard Speeches

Suicide Prevention: Saving Lives One Community at a Time

Suicide Prevention: Saving Lives One Community at a Time is a PowerPoint presentation with talking points.

The presentation provides an overview of the prevalence and risk factors for depression and suicide, dispels popular myths, and highlights AFSP's suicide prevention research and education programs. It includes practical advice for those who know someone who may be contemplating suicide.

Suicide Prevention: Saving Lives One Community at a Time

Suicide and the Elderly

Suicide and the Elderly is a PowerPoint presentation with talking points that addresses suicide among older adults. The presentation identifies key risk factors for suicide in the elderly, including depression and other psychiatric illnesses, and discusses treatment options.

Suicide and the Elderly

References

Books About Suicide

Reducing Suicide: A National Imperative

A thorough overview of the causes, prevention, and treatment of suicide in the United States written by an expert panel convened by the Institute of Medicine (IOM), an

independent, nonprofit organization that works outside of government to provide unbiased and authoritative advice to decision makers and the public. Available for purchase, or for free downloaded from the <u>National Academies Press website</u>.
Goldsmith S.K., Pellmar T.C., Kleinman A.M., & Bunney W.E. (Eds.). (2002). *Reducing Suicide: A National Imperative.* Washington, DC: National Academies Press.

Treating and Preventing Adolescent Mental Health Disorders

A groundbreaking survey of treatments and preventions written by a distinguished group of psychiatrists and clinical psychologists. The book addresses stigma and the role of primary-care providers in diagnosing and treating adolescent mental health problems. Available online, in bookstores, and available to read for free at the Oxford University Press website.

Evans D.L. Foa E.B. Gur R.E. Hendin H. O'Brien C.P. Seligman M.E. & Walsh B.T. (Eds.). (2005). *Treating and Preventing Adolescent Mental Health Disorders*. New York, NY: Oxford University Press.

- Publications from AFSP's Research
- Treatment
- Key Research Findings
- Adolescents Who Make Suicide Attempts Consider Risks Differently
- Coping with Suicide Loss
- Where Do I Begin?
- Find Support
- International Survivors of Suicide Loss Day
- Personal Stories
- Congressional Spouses for Suicide Prevention and Education
Contact Us

- **Out of the Darkness Walks**
  Community Walks
  Campus Walks
  The Overnight Walk
- **Local Chapters**
  Find Your Local Chapter
  Event Calendar

Used With Permission.